# Visual Guide to
# Grammar and Punctuation

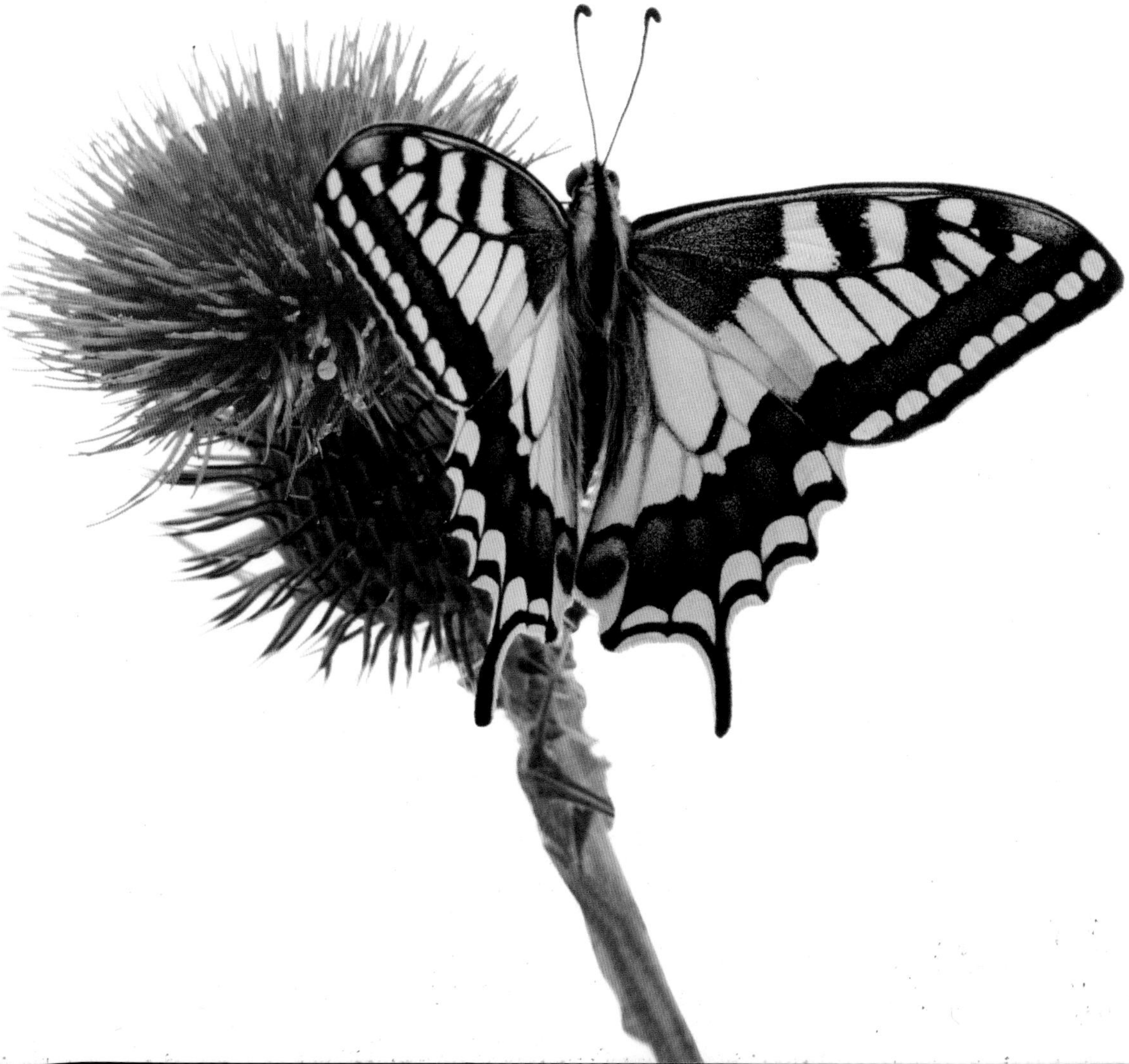

**Written by** Sheila Dignen
**Senior editor** Marie Greenwood
**Art editors** Shipra Jain, Seepiya Sahni
**Assistant editor** Anwesha Dutta
**DTP designer** Bimlesh Tiwary,
Nityanand Kumar
**Jacket co-ordinator** Francesca Young
**Jacket editor** Ishani Nandi
**Jacket designers** Amy Keast,
Dheeraj Arora
**Managing editors** Laura Gilbert,
Alka Thakur Hazarika
**Managing art editors** Diane Peyton Jones,
Romi Chakraborty
**CTS manager** Balwant Singh
**Production manager** Pankaj Sharma
**Picture researcher** Sakshi Saluja
**Pre-production producer** Dragana Puvacic
**Producer** Isabell Schart
**Art director** Martin Wilson
**Publisher** Sarah Larter
**Publishing director** Sophie Mitchell

A CIP catalogue record for this book is
available from the British Library.
ISBN: 978-0-2412-8384-4

Printed and bound in China

A WORLD OF IDEAS:
SEE ALL THERE IS TO KNOW
www.dk.com

# Contents

a small white dog
with a flowing cape

Elephants are **amazingly strong**.

The balloon **was going** higher and higher.

# Introduction

apostrophes

verbs

adjectives

auxiliary

clauses

ellipses

past tense

When you learn about the grammar of your own language, the most important thing to remember is that you already know most of it. Every time you open your mouth to speak, you are using grammar without even realizing it!

future tense

perfect tense

commas

adverbs

You talk about what you did yesterday and what you're going to do tomorrow; you talk about one friend, two friends or your brother's friends; you talk about exciting films, more exciting films and the most exciting film you've ever seen ...

pronouns

hyphens

capital

exclamations

colons

verb

direct speech

objects

noun phrases

questions

exclamation marks

infinitives

brackets

subjects

When you talk about all these things, you are using grammar. This book will teach you how to understand the different kinds of words in English, how they fit together to create different meanings and how to use punctuation correctly when you write.

full stops

Best of all, it will help you to have fun with language and become confident using it, so that you can choose the best words and the best kinds of sentences for what you want to say or write.

So let's get started!

letters

5

# How to use this book

There are different ways to read this book. You can either start at the beginning and work your way through, or you can dip into different topics. There are examples given for each topic, and each example is accompanied by a picture. We hope that you enjoy learning about the English language!

**How the pages work**
Each page or pair of pages introduces a new grammar or punctuation topic. The heading tells you what the topic is.

**Introduction**
Each topic is explained in the introduction, for example, how to use nouns or adjectives, or how to use commas. The word or punctuation mark being covered is shown in **bold**.

**Heading**

## Sentences

A **sentence** is a group of words that make sense on their own. A sentence might give information or ask a question. A sentence always begins with a capital letter, and it ends with a full stop, a question mark or an exclamation mark.

Look at these words, and see how they become a sentence.

| Giraffes | Giraffes have | Giraffes have long | Giraffes have long necks. |
|---|---|---|---|

| I want to | I want to travel to | I want to travel to the Moon | I want to travel to the Moon in a rocket. |
|---|---|---|---|

All sentences **must** have a verb. You can't make a sentence without a verb because the verb tells us what happens.

| I football every day. | I play football every day. | Snakes along the ground. | Snakes slither along the ground. |
|---|---|---|---|

## Adverbs

Verbs tell you what things **do**. For example, tigers **roar** and birds **sing**. **Adverbs** tell you how they do it. Most adverbs end in **-ly**, and they usually come after verbs. Adverbs that tell you how someone does something are called **adverbs of manner**.

The lion roared **fiercely**.

Some birds can sing **beautifully**.

She tiptoed **quietly** down the stairs.

The sun was shining **brightly**.

I won **easily**.

You have to balance them **carefully**.

Some adverbs don't end in **-ly**, but they are still adverb you how something is done.

We playe

I can run **fast**.

I always work **hard**.

You need to hold on **tight**.

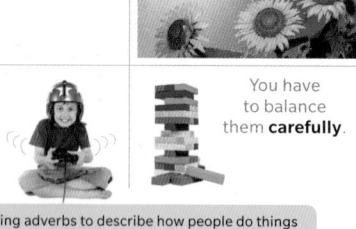

**Top tip** Using adverbs to describe how people do things can make your writing more lively and interesting.

46

70

47

**Remember!**
Without an adverb, you can smile,
Or ride a bike or sleep a while.
With adverbs, you smile **gleefully**,
Ride **skilfully**, sleep **peacefully**.

**Examples**
You will find lots of examples throughout. The relevant part of speech or punctuation is shown in **bold** or sometimes underlined.

**Top tips**
Handy tips are given to help you.

**Remember!**
Read the rhymes – they will help you remember those tricky points of grammar or punctuation.

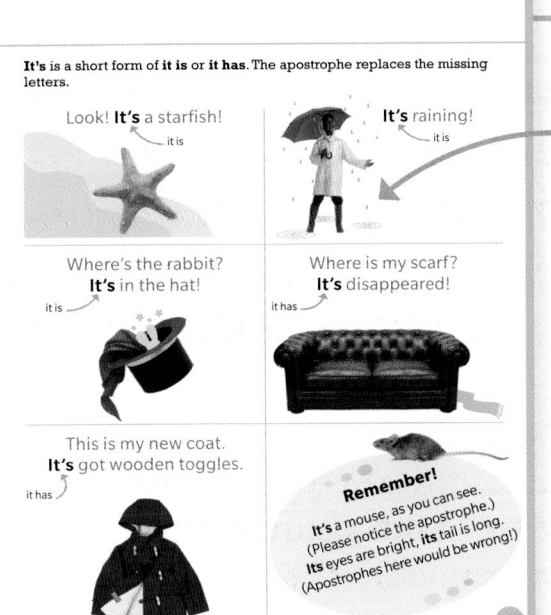

## Its or it's

You use **its**, with no apostrophe, to show that something belongs to an animal or a thing.

The dog is wagging **its** tail.

The baby monkey stays close to **its** mother.

The baby snake is coming out of **its** shell.

The bird is sitting on **its** eggs in **its** nest.

This bucket has lost **its** handle.

I can't play this now because **its** strings are broken.

**It's** is a short form of **it is** or **it has**. The apostrophe replaces the missing letters.

Look! **It's** a starfish!
it is

**It's** raining!
it is

Where's the rabbit? **It's** in the hat!
it is

Where is my scarf? **It's** disappeared!
it has

This is my new coat. **It's** got wooden toggles.
it has

**Remember!**
It's a mouse, as you can see. (Please notice the apostrophe.) Its eyes are bright, its tail is long. (Apostrophes here would be wrong!)

107

## Pictures
The example pictures help make the text easier to understand.

---

...es have a subject, which tells us who does the action

...etahs run fast.
verb

Beetles scuttle along.
subject  verb

...r thing that comes after the verb is called the object.
...ceives the action of the verb.

verb  object
...e love maths!
+ 7 = 12

subject  object
I read books.
verb

...s playing chess.
...ject  verb  object

Sasha is eating a banana.
subject  verb  object

71

---

## Three sections
The book has three sections: Parts of speech (blue); Sentences and clauses (orange); Punctuation (green). The colour tells you which section you are in.

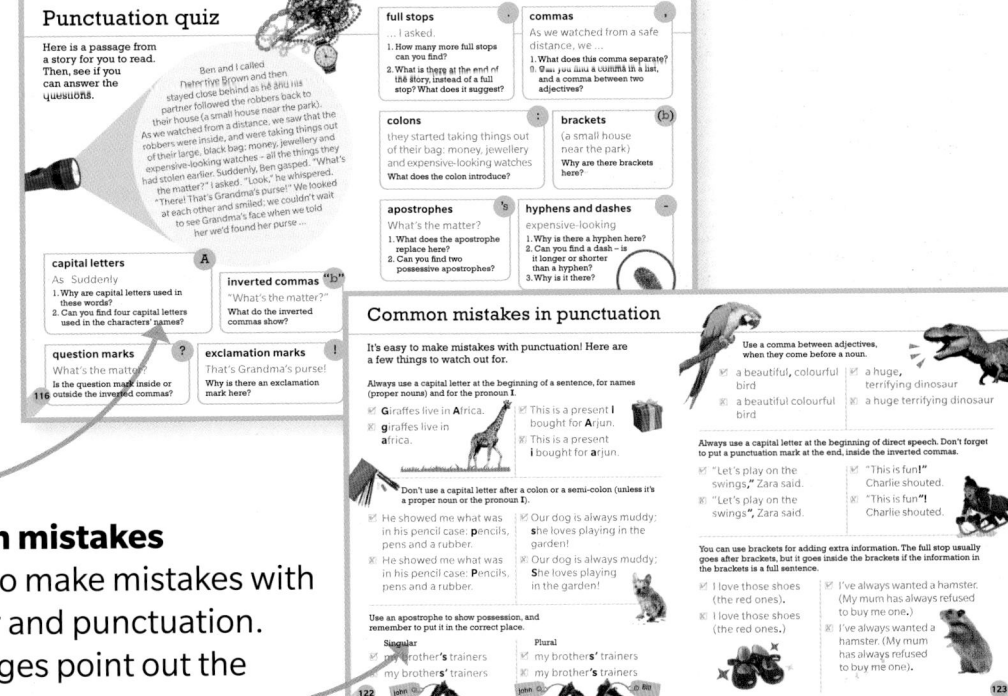

### Punctuation quiz

Here is a passage from a story for you to read. Then, see if you can answer the questions.

Ben and I called Detective Brown and then stayed close behind as he and his partner followed the robbers back to their house (a small house near the park). As we watched from a distance, we saw that the robbers were inside, and were taking things out of their large, black bag: money, jewellery and expensive-looking watches – all the things they had stolen earlier. Suddenly, Ben gasped. "What's the matter?" I asked. "Look," he whispered. "There! That's Grandma's purse!" We looked at each other and smiled; we couldn't wait to see Grandma's face when we told her we'd found her purse ...

**full stops** •
... I asked.
1. How many more full stops can you find?
2. What is there at the end of the story, instead of a full stop? What does it suggest?

**commas** ,
As we watched from a safe distance, we ...
1. What does this comma separate?
2. Can you find a comma in a list, and a comma between two adjectives?

**colons** :
they started taking things out of their bag: money, jewellery and expensive-looking watches
What does the colon introduce?

**brackets** (b)
(a small house near the park)
Why are there brackets here?

**apostrophes** 's
What's the matter?
1. What does the apostrophe replace here?
2. Can you find two possessive apostrophes?

**hyphens and dashes** -
expensive-looking
1. Why is there a hyphen here?
2. Can you find a dash – is it longer or shorter than a hyphen?
3. Why is it there?

**capital letters** A
As Suddenly
1. Why are capital letters used in these words?
2. Can you find four capital letters used in the characters' names?

**inverted commas** "b"
"What's the matter?"
What do the inverted commas show?

**question marks** ?
What's the matter?
Is the question mark inside or outside the inverted commas?

**exclamation marks** !
That's Grandma's purse!
Why is there an exclamation mark here?

116

### Common mistakes in punctuation

It's easy to make mistakes with punctuation! Here are a few things to watch out for.

Always use a capital letter at the beginning of a sentence, for names (proper nouns) and for the pronoun I.

✓ Giraffes live in Africa.
✗ giraffes live in africa.

✓ This is a present I bought for Arjun.
✗ This is a present i bought for arjun.

Don't use a capital letter after a colon or a semi-colon (unless it's a proper noun or the pronoun I).

✓ He showed me what was in his pencil case: pencils, pens and a rubber.
✗ He showed me what was in his pencil case: Pencils, pens and a rubber.

✓ Our dog is always muddy; she loves playing in the garden!
✗ Our dog is always muddy; She loves playing in the garden!

Use an apostrophe to show possession, and remember to put it in the correct place.

| Singular | Plural |
|---|---|
| ✓ my brother's trainers | ✓ my brothers' trainers |
| ✗ my brothers' trainers | ✗ my brother's trainers |

Use a comma between adjectives, when they come before a noun.

✓ a beautiful, colourful bird
✗ a beautiful colourful bird

✓ a huge, terrifying dinosaur
✗ a huge terrifying dinosaur

Always use a capital letter at the beginning of direct speech. Don't forget to put a punctuation mark at the end, inside the inverted commas.

✓ "Let's play on the swings," Zara said.
✗ "Let's play on the swings", Zara said.

✓ "This is fun!" Charlie shouted.
✗ "This is fun" Charlie shouted.

You can use brackets for adding extra information. The full stop usually goes after brackets, but it goes inside the brackets if the information in the brackets is a full sentence.

✓ I love those shoes (the red ones).
✗ I love those shoes (the red ones.)

✓ I've always wanted a hamster. (My mum has always refused to buy me one.)
✗ I've always wanted a hamster. (My mum has always refused to buy me one).

122   123

## Quizzes
Try the quizzes and see if you can answer the questions. There's a quiz at the end of each section.

## Common mistakes
It's easy to make mistakes with grammar and punctuation. These pages point out the most common ones.

# What is grammar?

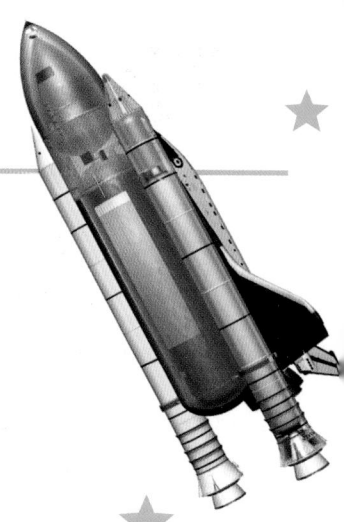

We use words when we talk to and write to each other. There are thousands of different words in any language, and they all have their own meanings. **Grammar** is the way we put these words together so that they make sense.

Words scattered about on their own don't mean very much.

huge    to    zoomed    planet    up

An    a    rocket

into    distant    space

alien    travelled

The

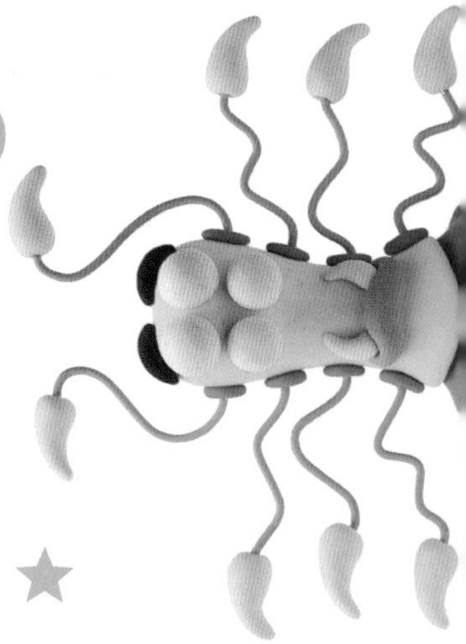

Words are like pieces of a jigsaw. We need to fit them together to make meaning.

The  huge  rocket  zoomed  up  into  space

An  alien  travelled  to  a  distant  planet

8

# What is punctuation?

When speaking, you might pause when you've finished saying something or you might shout if you are angry. When you write, you use **punctuation** to make your meaning clear. You show the reader when to pause, when something is a question or when something is shouted.

With no punctuation, a sentence is hard to understand.

the toy shop was amazing there were shelves packed with all kinds of exciting things wooden trains action figures brightly coloured kites and lots more

We need to add punctuation to make the meaning clear.

The toy shop was amazing! There were shelves packed with all kinds of exciting things: wooden trains, action figures, brightly coloured kites and lots more.

Sometimes punctuation can change the meaning of a sentence.

We found gold coins and jewels.

We found gold, coins and jewels.

9

## Prepositions

The astronaut flew **to** the Moon **in** a rocket.

## Adjectives

a **green** and **yellow** parrot

## Verbs

roar

hunt

## Conjunctions

## Nouns

He's a **wizard**.

Most animals look cute **when** they are young.

## Pronouns

**My** sister wants to be a vet.

Mum bought **her** a kitten.

Wasps can sting you. **Ouch!**

## Interjections

## Adverb

I can run **fast**.

# Parts of speech

## Determiners

Look at **the** penguins!

## Tenses

It **snowed** last night.

# Nouns

The things, animals and people in the world around us all have names. These names are called **nouns**.

tree

leaf

branch

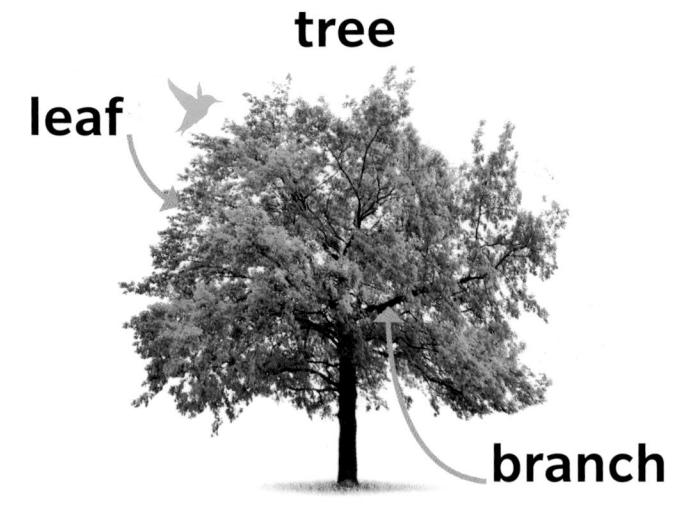

tiger

stripes

fur

castle

tower

window

tractor

cab

wheel

dinosaur

tail

claw

**Remember!**

Every thing has a name,
And every name is a noun.
From a **mouse** to a **mountain**,
From a **castle** to a **clown**.

12

The nouns on these two pages are called **common nouns** because they don't talk about one specific thing or person. You can use the noun **tree** about any tree, and the noun **brother** about anyone's brother.

This is my
**brother**.

She's a
**teacher**.

He's a
**singer**.

I'm the
**champion**.

There are also nouns for things that aren't real,
but only exist in our imagination.

He's a **wizard**.

Here's a **dragon**.

# Proper nouns

A **proper noun** is the name of an actual person or place.
A proper noun always begins with a capital letter.

Some proper nouns are the names of people:

**Emily**    **Jack**

**Cindy Adams**

Some proper nouns are the names of countries, cities or towns:

**France**

**New York City**

The names of months and days of the week are also proper nouns:

We go on holiday in **August**.

We start school on **Monday**.

# Abstract nouns

**Abstract nouns** are names for things you can't see, hear or touch.

health

hunger

Some abstract nouns are feelings:

happiness

disappointment

Some abstract nouns are ideas:

speed

fame

# Singular and plural nouns

A **singular noun** talks about just one thing. A **plural noun** is used for more than one thing. With most nouns, we add -**s** to the end of the word to make the plural.

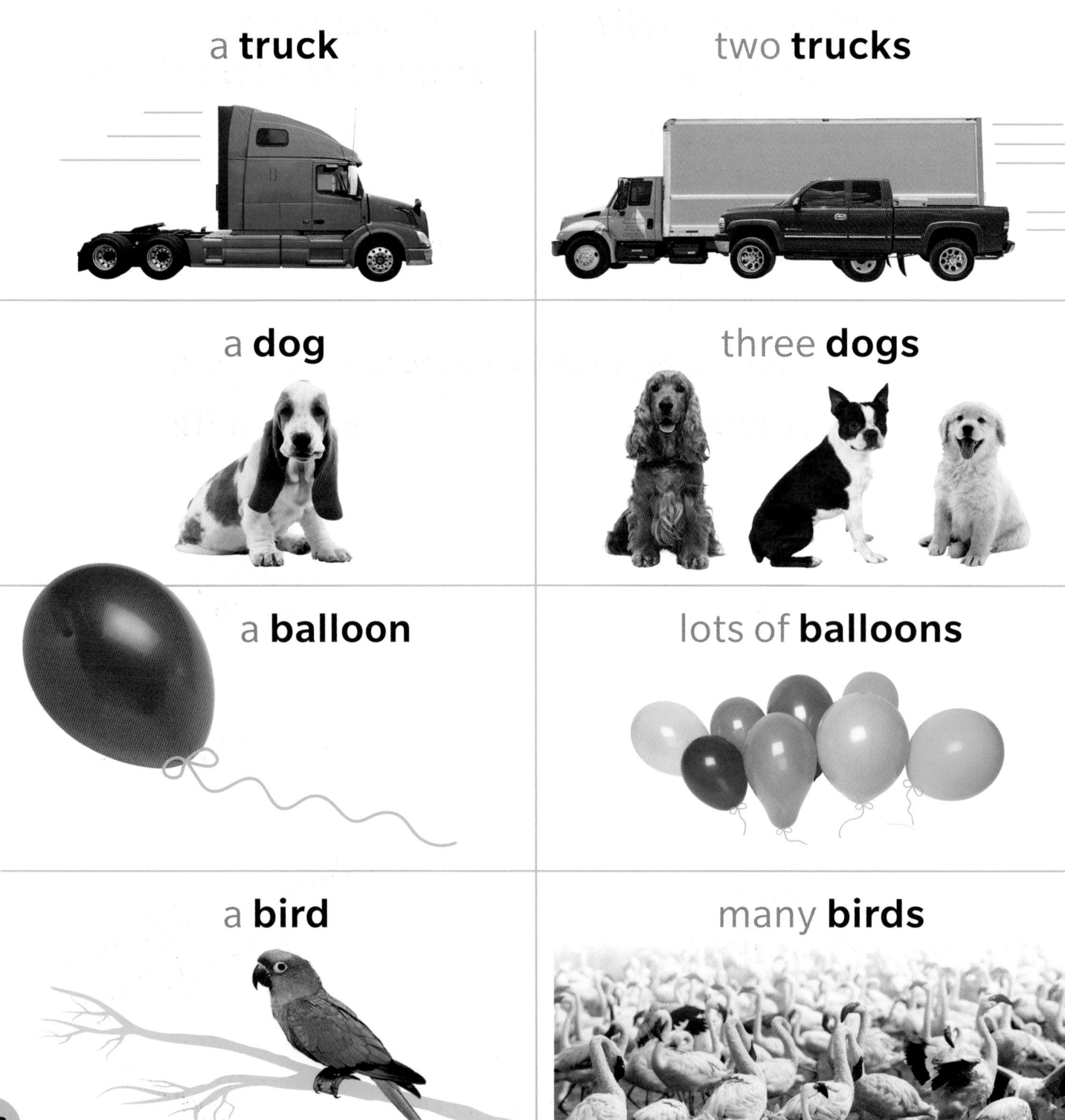

| a **truck** | two **trucks** |
| a **dog** | three **dogs** |
| a **balloon** | lots of **balloons** |
| a **bird** | many **birds** |

Nouns that have a singular and plural are called **countable** nouns. This means we can count them. Some nouns don't have a plural. These are called **uncountable** nouns.

one **pencil**, two **pencils**, three **pencils**

One **cherry** for you, and two **cherries** for me!

These are **uncountable** nouns, because you cannot count them:

some **furniture**

some **milk**

lots of **money**

some loud **music**

**Top tip** Uncountable nouns don't have a plural. We can't say "two furnitures" or "lots of moneys".

# Compound nouns

We sometimes put words together to make new nouns. These nouns are called **compound nouns**.

rain + coat = **raincoat**

star + fish = **starfish**

cup + cake = **cupcake**

sun + rise = **sunrise**

hand + bag = **handbag**

tooth + paste = **toothpaste**

tooth + brush = **toothbrush**

# Collective nouns

Some nouns refer to a group of animals, people or things. They are called **collective nouns**.

a **flock** of geese

a **herd** of elephants

a **team** of hockey players

a **range** of mountains

a **fleet** of fishing boats

a **school** of fish

# Verbs

**Verbs** tell you what things, or nouns, **do**. They are sometimes called "doing words". Look at what these people, animals and things can do.

walk

roar

hunt

dance

turn

spin

fly

zoom

take off

bang

pop

whizz

play

lose

win

climb    swing

balance

Here are some nouns with verbs added to show what each noun is doing.

Crocodiles **hunt**.

An ice-skater **spins** round and round.

Owls **fly**.

A scooter **whizzes** by.

The gymnast **balances**.

**Remember!**

A noun on its own
Is just a thing.
A verb makes it **run**,
And **dance** and **sing**!

21

# Verbs and subjects

Verbs describe actions, such as **run**, **jump** and **play**. The person or thing that **does** the action of the verb is the **subject**. The subject always comes before the verb.

The **athlete** jumps.

The **clown** juggles.

The **butterfly** lands.

The **boat** sails.

The **star** twinkles.

The **rain** falls.

Sometimes the verb has to change a little to match the subject. We add **-s** or **-es** to the end of the verb if the subject is a single thing that you can call **he**, **she** or **it**.

All dogs **bark**.

This dog **barks** a lot.

He **barks** a lot.

Trains **go** fast.

This train **goes** slowly.

It **goes** slowly.

Some verbs change in different ways to match the subject.

This car **is** red.

These cars **are** red.

# Subjects and objects

The **subject** of a verb comes before the verb. It tells you who or what **does** the action of the verb. Some verbs need something else after them, otherwise the sentence doesn't make sense. The person or thing that comes after the verb is called the **object**. The object tells you who or what receives the action of the verb.

The **dog** chased...
subject
?

**Ella** saw...
subject
?

The **dog** chased a **ball**.
subject    object

**Ella** saw her **mum**.
subject    object

Some verbs don't need an object and make sense on their own.

The **tiger** roars.
subject

**Flowers** grow.
subject

24

With some verbs, there is a choice. Sometimes they have an object, and sometimes they don't. But the subject always comes before the verb.

All **kittens** play.

subject

subject
Some **kittens**
play **catch**.

object

All **animals** eat.

subject

subject
**Orangutans**
eat **apples**.

object

Remember, the subject comes first …

The **cat** chases the **mouse**!

… otherwise you get the
wrong meaning!

**Remember!**

If **cats chase mice**, I do declare,
Then cats are **subjects**, fair and square.
The mice are **objects**, by the way,
And if they're fast, they'll get away!

25

# The verb be

The verb **be** isn't like other verbs. It is irregular, which means it has its own rules. It takes lots of different forms, such as **am**, **are** and **is**.

I **am** hungry!

You **are** my friend!

That elephant **is** huge!

These snakes **are** scary!

Please **be** quiet!

He's **being** helpful.

After the verb **be**, we can use a noun, to say what something is, or we can use an adjective, to say what it is like.

This **is** a tiger.
It **is** fierce.

He **is** a clown.
He **is** funny.

We **are** the champions.
We **are** proud!

These **are** rhinos.
They **are** strong.

We can also use the verb **be** to talk about the past.
We use the forms **was** and **were**.

Yesterday
I **was** seven.

Today
I **am** eight.

Last week
we **were**
on holiday.

Now we **are**
back home!

27

# Pronouns

Sometimes we don't want to keep repeating the same noun over and over again. Instead, we can use a **pronoun** to replace the noun.

**Freddie** is a fast runner.

~~Freddie~~ **He** always wins.

One day I want to beat ~~Freddie~~ **him**.

**My sister** wants to be a vet.

**She** loves animals.

Mum bought **her** a kitten.

My little **brother's bike** is broken.

**He** is going to mend **it**.

**Owls** hunt when **they** are hungry.

Small animals try to get away from **them**.

**I**, **me** and **you** are also pronouns. We use them instead of using our own name or someone else's name.

Please can **I** have another biscuit?

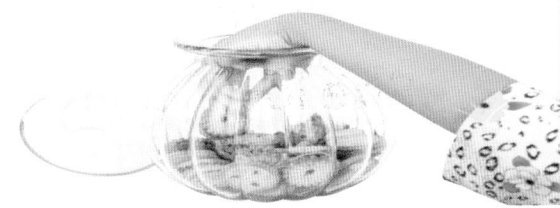

Can **you** teach **me** how to skateboard?

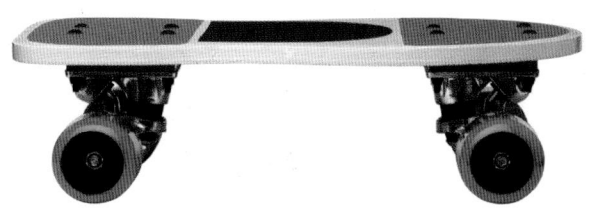

Words like **nothing**, **everything**, **nobody** and **somebody** are also pronouns.

There's **nothing** in my case.

I want to invite **everybody** to my party.

Dear Aiden, Please come to my party.

**Nobody** answered the door.

**Somebody** has eaten the pizza.

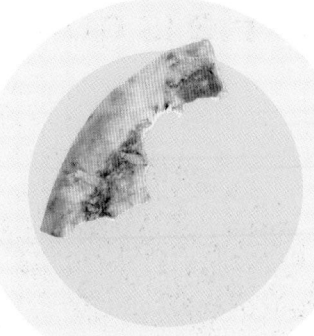

**Top tip**
When I is used as a pronoun, always write it as a capital letter.

# I or me?

Always use **I**, not **me**, before a verb. This rule is the same whether you are talking about just yourself, or you and someone else.

I watched a film.

**Adam and I** watched a film.

I found some buried treasure.

**Elsie and I** found some buried treasure.

People sometimes say "**Me and Adam** watched a film."
However, this isn't correct – you would never say "**Me** watched a film."

Use **me** in other parts of a sentence:

The bull chased **me**.

The bull chased **Ali and me**.

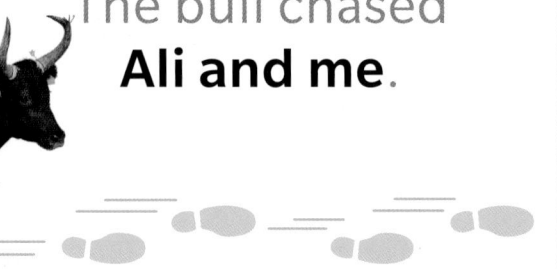

Are those apples for **me**?

Are those apples for **Rosa and me**?

**Remember!**

**Lily and I** sailed out to sea.
What an adventure for **Lily and me**!

**Top tip**

It's polite to put the other person first.
Say **Tom and I** or **Tom and me**.

# Possessive pronouns

You can use **possessive pronouns** to say who something belongs to. Possessive pronouns replace the noun.

This ball is ~~my ball~~ **mine**.

Is that bike **yours**?

Tom says those gloves are **his**.

I gave my old boots to my sister, so they're **hers** now.

These bananas are **ours**.

We'll clear up our mess, and they can clear up **theirs**.

**Top tip**

Here are six possessive pronouns:
**mine**, **yours**, **his**, **hers**, **ours**, **theirs**.

# Present and past tenses

Some things happen right now, in the present. Some things happened in the past. Different forms of a verb show when something happens. These are called **tenses**.

We use the **present tense** for things that happen now, every day, or every time. We use the **past tense** for things that happened in the past.

These are in the present:

It **snows** in winter.

We **plant** flowers each year.

These are in the past:

It **snowed** last night.

We **planted** some flowers last year.

With a lot of verbs, we add -**ed** at the end to make the past tense, but some verbs change completely.

This is in the present:

I always **win**.

This is in the past:

I **won** the race.

# Future tense

No one really knows what will happen in the future, but we like talking about it. We can use **will** and **won't** (will not) if we feel sure about something in the future.

Of course I **will** win the race.

I definitely **won't** go to Mars.

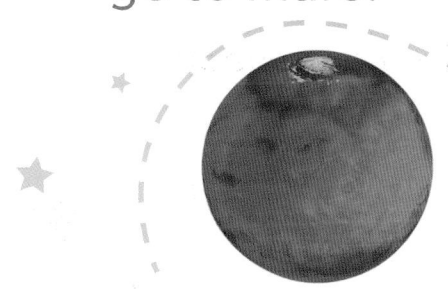

We can use **might** or **may** if we're not so sure that something will happen.

The cat **might** catch the bird.

I **may** share my toys.

We can also say that we are **going to** do something in the future, if that's what we are planning to do.

I'm **going to** ride a bike.

I'm **going to** paint a a room.

# Progressive tenses

We use different tenses to say whether something happens in the present, past or future. Sometimes we want to say that something isn't finished or it goes on for a long time. For this, we use the **progressive tense**.

We use the **present progressive** to say that something is happening right now.

He **is making** a sandcastle.

We **are skating** on the ice.

The dog **is burying** a bone.

The animals **are drinking**.

We use the normal present tense for things that happen every day or every week. However, we use the present progressive for something that is happening right now.

I **make** ← present
something different every week.

Today, I **am making** a robot.
present progressive

34

We use the **past progressive** for things that kept happening for a while. We often use the past progressive to show that something else was happening at the same time.

I **was starting** to feel a bit sick!

The balloon **was going** higher and higher.

The fireworks **were making** a lot of noise.

I **was riding** my bike in the park, when a puppy ran out in front of me.

We use the past tense for things that happened and finished in the past. We use the past progressive for things that kept happening for a while.

The cat **climbed** to the top of the tree.

past

The cat **was climbing** up the tree.

past progressive

**Top tip**
The progressive form of a verb always ends in **-ing**.

35

# Perfect tenses

The **perfect tenses** are two more tenses that we can use to talk about the past.

We use the **present perfect** when we are talking about something that happened in the past, but we are thinking about what it means **now**.

**I have finished** my homework!

The squirrel **has found** some nuts.

Look at the difference between the present perfect and the past tense:

**I have lost** my phone.

present perfect

**I lost** my phone, but my dad bought me a new one.

past

The dog **has gone** into the garden.

present perfect

The dog **went** into the garden and got very muddy!

past

In stories, we usually say what happened first, what happened next and what happened in the end. If we talk about something that happened earlier on, we use the **past perfect**.

We walked all day, and in the evening, we arrived at the gates of an old house. It was all quiet, and my companions wanted to go in. But my uncle **had warned** me that it was dangerous.

past perfect

This means my uncle warned me earlier, before we set out.

The professor opened the door to the laboratory and went in. He looked around, and listened carefully – nothing. With a feeling of horror, he realized that it was true. The dinosaurs **had escaped**!

past perfect

This means the dinosaurs escaped earlier, before the professor got to the laboratory.

37

# Auxiliary verbs

We use different tenses, such as the past tense and the present tense. We use verbs called **auxiliary verbs**, or "helping verbs", to help us make all the other different tenses.

Look at the sentences below. See how the auxiliary verbs **have** and **be** slightly change the meaning of the sentences and form new tenses.

The dog **ate** my sandwiches! — past tense

The dog **has eaten** my sandwiches! — present perfect

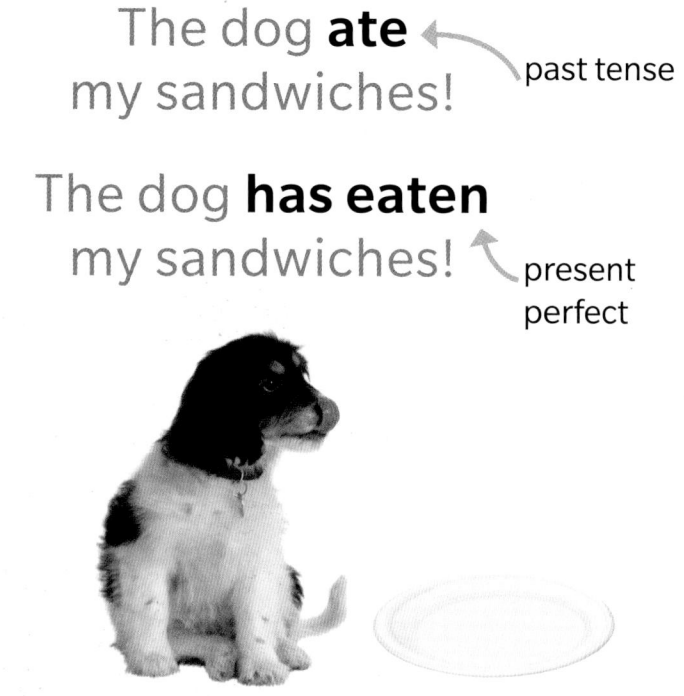

Horses **eat** grass. — present tense

The horses **are eating** grass. — present progressive

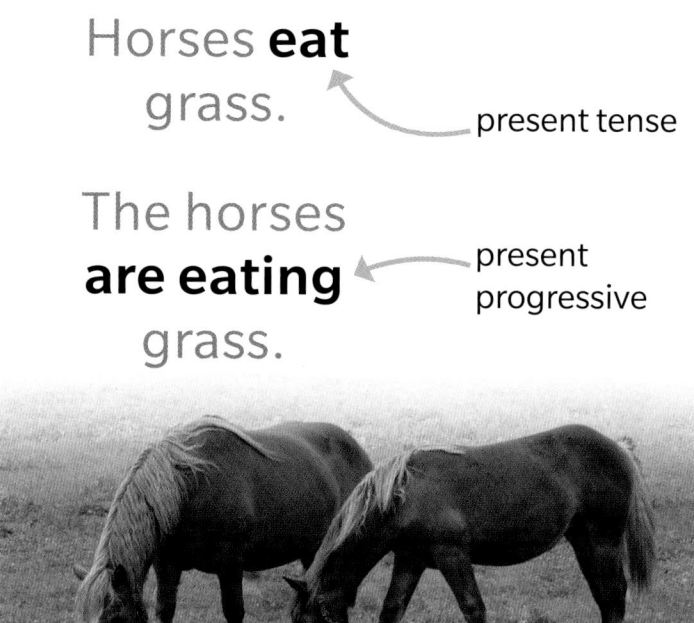

We use the verb **be** as an auxiliary verb in progressive tenses.

He **is learning** to juggle.

**Are** you **winning**?

We use the verb **do** as an auxiliary verb in the present tense. It helps us to make questions, or to make sentences negative.

I like milkshakes. **Do** you **like** milkshakes too?

We play tennis in the summer. We **don't play** football.

**Did** is the past tense of **do**. We use this as an auxiliary verb in the past tenses.

I enjoyed our day at the safari park. **Did** you **enjoy** it?

We found a few old tools, but we **didn't find** any toys.

We use **have** as an auxiliary verb in the present perfect.

We **have made** some lemonade.

The plane **hasn't taken off** yet.

# Infinitives

The **infinitive** of a verb is the name of the verb, such as **eat**, **play** or **sleep**. It hasn't been changed to make different tenses. When you look up a verb in a dictionary, you look up the infinitive.

You can use the infinitive after **to**:

The witch decided **to make** a magic potion.

The monkey needs **to hold** on tight.

I don't want **to go** home!

We set off **to explore** the forest.

Would you like **to stay** for lunch?

The bird is trying **to balance**.

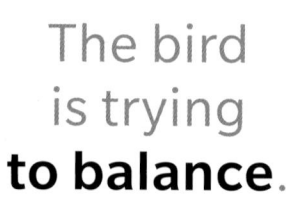

We also use the infinitive after verbs such as **can**, **will**, **might** and **must**. These verbs are called **modal verbs**.

I **can walk** on my hands.

I **might have** fish for dinner.

You **must pass** the ball.

You **should eat** plenty of fruit.

The spider hopes a fly **will come** along soon!

Don't worry, it **won't hurt**.

# Adjectives

**Adjectives** tell us what people, animals and things are like. They describe nouns and tell you more about them. They might tell you what things look, sound or feel like.

fierce

stripy

strong

mysterious

magical

haunted

obedient

friendly

noisy

comfortable

expensive

fast

colourful

beautiful

delicate

**Remember!**

Adjectives make lions **strong**, And rockets **fast** and rivers **long**.

42

Some adjectives describe the colour of something:

a **blue** and **yellow** hat with **red** pompoms

a **green** and **yellow** parrot

Some adjectives describe size or shape:

a **small** beetle with **big** jaws

a **triangular** piece of pizza on a **round** plate

Some adjectives describe feelings:

She's **content** and **relaxed**.

He's **happy** and **excited**.

43

# Where to put adjectives

We often put an adjective **before** the noun that it is describing.

a **colourful** ball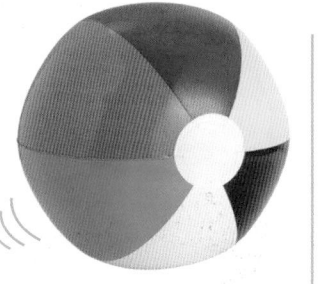

a **huge** spider

You can also put adjectives **after** the noun, such as after verbs like **be**, **look** or **feel**.

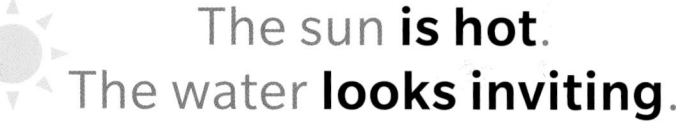 The sun **is hot**.
The water **looks inviting**.

Our cat **is lovely**.
His fur **feels soft**.

It's up to you to choose where you put the adjectives in your sentence.

This is a **delicious** salad.
This salad is **delicious**.

We saw some **amazing** fireworks.
The fireworks were **amazing**.

You can use more than one adjective to describe something. When you put two adjectives **before** a noun, you usually need to use a comma.

some **beautiful**, **delicate** flowers

a **large**, **ferocious** crocodile

When you use two adjectives **after** a noun, you join them with **and**.

A rabbit's ears are **long and pointed**.

The roller coaster was **fast and scary**.

If you're using more than one adjective, think about the best order for them. Sometimes they don't sound quite right if you put them in the wrong order.

☑ It's got small, black spots.

☒ It's got black, small spots.

☑ She's wearing a lovely, woolly jumper.

☒ She's wearing a woolly, lovely jumper.

Here, the sentence sounds better if the size comes first, then the colour.

Here, it sounds better if your opinion comes first (in this case that the jumper is lovely).

# Adverbs

Verbs tell you what things **do**. For example, tigers **roar** and birds **sing**. **Adverbs** tell you how they do it. Most adverbs end in **-ly**, and they usually come after verbs. Adverbs that tell you how someone does something are called **adverbs of manner**.

The lion roared **fiercely**.

Some birds can sing **beautifully**.

She tiptoed **quietly** down the stairs.

The sun was shining **brightly**.

I won **easily**.

You have to balance them **carefully**.

**Top tip** Using adverbs to describe how people do things can make your writing more lively and interesting.

Some adverbs don't end in **-ly**, but they are still adverbs if they tell you how something is done.

I can run **fast**.

We played **well** today.

I always work **hard**.

You need to hold on **tight**.

**Remember!**

Without an adverb, you can smile,
Or ride a bike or sleep a while.
With adverbs, you smile **gleefully**,
Ride **skilfully**, sleep **peacefully**.

# Adjectives into adverbs

We can change most adjectives into adverbs by adding **-ly** to the end of the adjective.

Snails are **slow** movers. They move **slowly**.

Anika is an **elegant** dancer. She dances **elegantly**.

If an adjective already ends in **-l**, we still add another one, so the adverb has a double **l**.

Sam gave me a **cheerful** smile. He smiled **cheerfully**.

The puppy gave a **playful** bark. He barked **playfully**.

If an adjective ends in **-y**, we change the ending to **-ily**.

The crocodile looked **hungry**. He looked at me **hungrily**.

We had a **happy** day on the beach. We played **happily** all day.

# Adverbs of place

Some adverbs tell us **where** something happens. These are called **adverbs of place**, and they don't usually end in **-ly**.

Pickles, come **here**!

We can sit **there**.

I've looked **everywhere**, but I can't find my gloves.

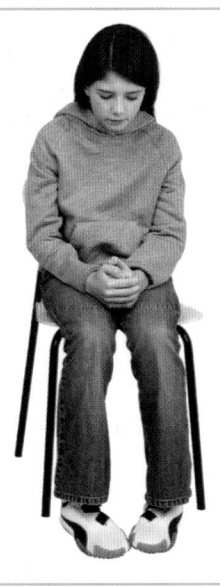

It's raining. Let's go **indoors**.

The dog ran **upstairs**.

Can you skateboard **backwards**?

# Adverbs of time

Some adverbs tell us **when** something happens. These are called **adverbs of time**.

It's my birthday **today**.

I got some new roller skates **yesterday**.

We're going on holiday **tomorrow**.

I don't want to do my homework **now**. I'll do it **later**!

Badgers **usually** sleep during the day.

She's **always** trying to catch the fish, but she **never** manages to!

# Adverbs before adjectives

We can use some adverbs before adjectives, to change the meaning of the adjective slightly. See how these adverbs change the meaning of the adjective **strong**.

Dogs are **fairly** **strong**.

Grizzly bears are **very** **strong**.

Gorillas are **extremely** **strong**.

Elephants are **amazingly** **strong**.

We often use these kinds of adverbs to emphasize or exaggerate something.

This book is **unbelievably exciting**!

The apple was **deliciously sweet**.

Sometimes, adverbs make a comment on the sentence. You can use adverbs to give your opinion. We often use them at the beginning of a sentence.

**Luckily,** I found my mobile phone under my bed.

DO NOT FEED THE MONKEYS! Thank you

**Unfortunately,** we couldn't feed the monkeys.

# Comparatives and superlatives

Sometimes we might want to compare people or things to say how they are different. We use **comparatives** and **superlatives** to do this.

expensive

**more** expensive

**most** expensive

heavy        heavier        heaviest

---

We use comparatives to compare two people or things.

A train is **faster** than a bike.

A lion is **more dangerous** than a mouse.

---

We use superlatives to compare three or more people or things.

A plane is the **fastest**.

A tiger is the **most dangerous**.

With short adjectives, we add -**er** to make comparatives and -**est** to make superlatives.

A camel is **slower** than a gazelle.

A tortoise is the **slowest**.

With longer adjectives, we use **more** to make comparatives and **most** to make superlatives.

Ice-skating is **more difficult** than riding a scooter.

Walking on a tightrope is the **most difficult**.

The adjectives **good** and **bad** have irregular comparatives and superlatives. This means they take different forms.

★ a **good** mark

★★ a **better** mark

★★★ the **best** mark you can get

My sister's socks smell really **bad**.

My dad's socks smell even **worse**.

My brother's socks smell the **worst** of all!

53

# Prepositions

We use **prepositions** to show how different nouns relate to each other in a sentence. Prepositions are small words, such as **on**, **in**, **to** and **with**.

See how prepositions link the nouns and pronouns in these sentences:

dog     ball     garden

The dog is playing **with** a ball **in** the garden.

I     castle     secret passage

I got **into** the castle **through** a secret passage.

astronaut     Moon     rocket

The astronaut flew **to** the Moon **in** a rocket.

Mum     cake     me     birthday

Mum made a cake **for** me **on** my birthday.

**Remember!**

**Up** the ladder and **over** the wall,
**Through** the door and **along** the hall,
**On** your skates or **with** a ball,
Prepositions link them all.

54

# Prepositions of place

Some prepositions tell us **where** something is or which direction it goes in.

The rabbit is **in** the basket.

The books are **on** the table.

He's diving **under** the water.

Can you find your way **through** the maze?

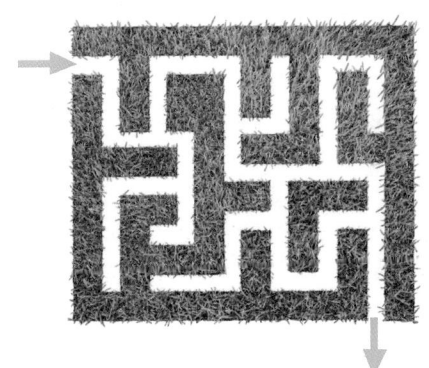

The horse jumped **over** the fence.

The squirrel is running **along** the branch.

# Prepositions of time

Some prepositions tell us **when** something happens.

We sometimes go camping **in** the summer.

We play music **on** Thursdays.

We don't go to school **at** the weekend.

Bats sleep **during** the day and come out **at** night.

My boots are always clean **before** the game.

We're going swimming **after** lunch.

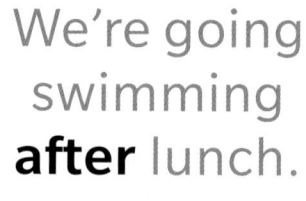

# Other prepositions

Some prepositions link nouns in other ways.

I tied my hair up **with** ribbons.

We gave some carrots **to** our rabbit.

I love travelling **by** train.

You can't go outside **without** your shoes.

I love books **about** teddy bears.

I'm making a card **for** my grandma.

# Conjunctions

Some sentences are quite simple and only give one idea. If you want to join more than one idea together in the same sentence, you can use a **conjunction** to link the ideas.

Lions live in Africa. They hunt for food.

Lions live in Africa **and** they hunt for food.

Let's go outside. It's warm and sunny!

Let's go outside **because** it's warm and sunny!

Each idea that you link together with a conjunction is called a clause.

We could play tennis **or** we could ride our bikes.

Most animals look cute **when** they are young.

**Remember!**
**And**, **but**, **because** or **so**,
Conjunctions link clauses, so now you know!

58

You can use prepositions to link nouns or pronouns into a sentence. Prepositions are followed by nouns. Conjunctions are different, because they can link whole clauses.

I was shivering **with** cold.

preposition    noun

I was shivering **because** it was cold.

conjunction    clause

You can't play on your tablet **during** lessons.

preposition    noun

You can't play on your tablet **when** you're in lessons.

conjunction    clause

Sometimes the same word can be both a preposition **and** a conjunction.

We'll go to the beach **after** lunch.

preposition    noun

We'll go to the beach **after** we've had lunch.

conjunction    clause

# Coordinating conjunctions

The conjunctions **and**, **but** and **or** are called **coordinating conjunctions** because they link words, phrases and clauses that are equally important.

I got 10 out of 10 in a test **and** I got a star!

Whales live in the oceans **and** they mainly eat fish.

I like tennis, **but** my brother prefers football.

I wanted a kitten, **but** my mum said no!

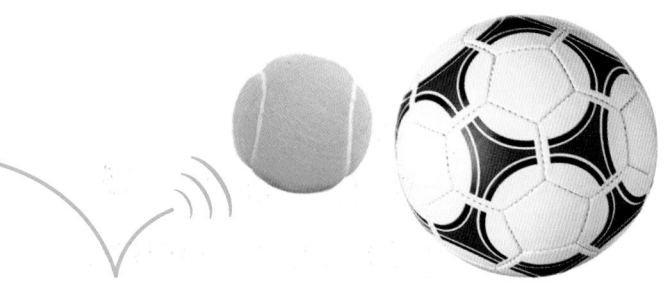

Shall we play a video game **or** go to the park?

Would you like an apple **or** a banana?

# Subordinating conjunctions

Conjunctions that **aren't** coordinating conjunctions are called **subordinating conjunctions**. They link a subordinate (less important) clause to a main clause. The subordinate clause often gives a reason for something, says when something happens or gives extra information.

You can't go on that ride **because** you're too small.

Tigers only hunt **when** they are hungry.

We've been friends **since** we were three.

I felt excited **as** I opened the door.

You can have some pizza **if** you're hungry.

I love Barney, **although** he is very grumpy-looking!

61

# Interjections

An **interjection** is a single word that expresses a thought or feeling. You often shout or say interjections loudly, and so they are often followed by an exclamation mark.

 **Hello!** We're over here.

 **Bye!** See you later!

**Thanks!** Can I open it now?

**Congratulations!** You won!

**Shh!** Don't make any noise.

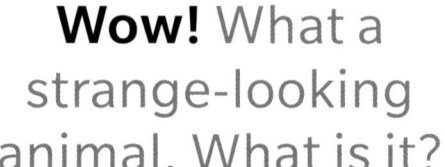

**Wow!** What a strange-looking animal. What is it?

(It's a Malayan tapir!)

We often use interjections to show how we are feeling.

**Brrr!**
I'm cold.

**Hooray!**
It's sports day.

**Ugh!**
A spider!

**Hey!** That's my
ball! Give it back!

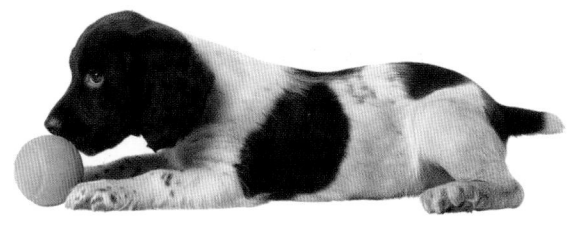

Wasps can
sting you.
**Ouch!**

**Oops!**
It broke.

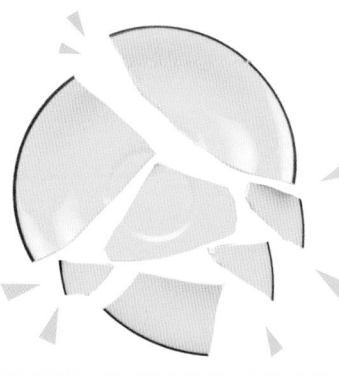

**Remember!**
**Hi! Hello!**
If you want my attention ...
**Wow! Hooray!**
Use an interjection!

# Determiners

Nouns are words for things, animals and people. **Determiners** are words that go before nouns. They tell you which thing or person you are talking about.

The words **a**, **an** and **the** are determiners. They are also sometimes called articles.

It's **a** horse.

Look at **the** penguins!

The words **this**, **that**, **these** and **those** are also determiners.

**This** ice lolly is delicious!

Look at **those** fish!

Numbers are determiners, too:

I've got **six** pencils.

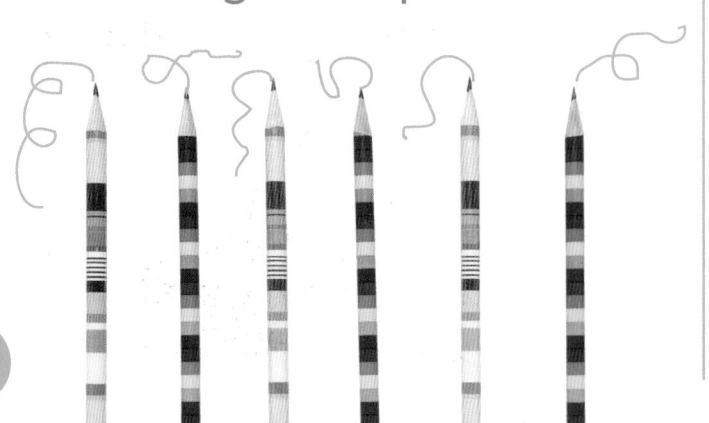

There are **five** puppies.

Words like **some**, **any** and **many** are determiners. We use them to talk about amounts of things, but without saying exactly how many there are.

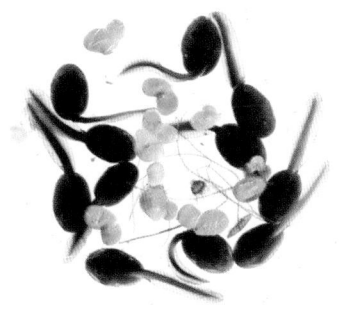

There are **some** tadpoles in the pond.

There aren't **many** clouds in the sky.

Some determiners tell us who something belongs to. These are called possessive determiners. The possessive determiners are: **my**, **your**, **his**, **her**, **its**, **our**, **their**.

**My** hair is getting quite long.

**Their** sandcastle is amazing!

Adjectives can come before nouns, to describe them. Determiners always come before adjectives.

Look at **that little** pony!

determiner ⤴ ⤴ adjective

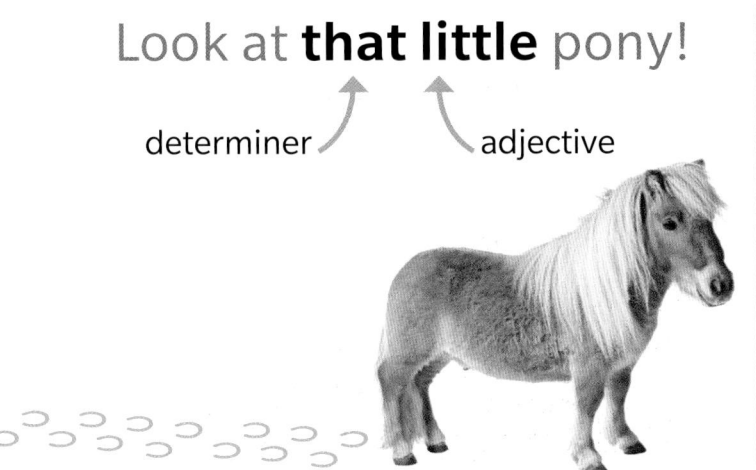

Do you like **my new** shoes?

determiner ⤴ ⤴ adjective

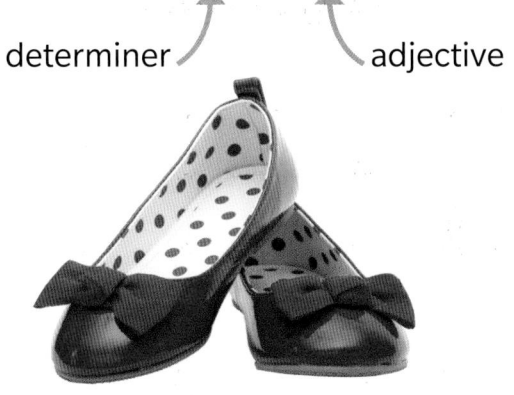

# Parts of speech quiz

Here is a passage from a story for you to read. Then, see if you can answer the questions below. You'll find the answers on the next page.

It was getting dark, and the animals in the jungle were slowly beginning to stir. The tiger opened one eye, then stretched and yawned lazily. He was feeling hungry, because he hadn't eaten for two days. He looked up at the moonlit sky above. The Moon was small and pale, so there wasn't much light. Yes! It would be a perfect night for hunting!

## nouns
tiger  Moon

How many more nouns can you find?

## verbs
stretched  would be

Can you find 11 more verbs in the story? (Don't forget to include different forms of the verb **be**.)

## pronouns
it

Can you find the pronoun that replaces the word **tiger**?

## adjectives
dark  hungry

Can you find four more adjectives in the story?

## tenses

### was getting opened

1. What tense is **was getting** and **were beginning**?
2. Can you find four verbs in the past tense, and one verb in the past perfect?

## adverbs

### slowly only

1. Can you find one more adverb of manner?
2. Can you find one adverb of place, and one adverb of time?

## conjunctions

### and

1. Is **and** a coordinating conjunction or a subordinating conjunction?
2. Can you find two subordinating conjunctions?

## prepositions

### in

Can you find two more prepositions?

## interjections

Can you find one interjection?

## determiners

### a the much

Can you find two numbers that are determiners?

# Exclamations

How scary!

"What's in your bag?"

Molly asked me what was in my bag.

## Direct speech and Reported speech

## Questions

Do you like oranges?

# Commands

Mix the flour and the butter.

## Sentences

Giraffes have long necks.

## Statements

Pumpkins are tasty, and you can also use them to make lanterns.

## Adverbials

He fought **bravely**.

He fought **with great courage**.

## Noun phrases

a small white dog with a little orange collar

# Sentences, phrases and clauses

## Active and passive sentences

**Noah** caught the ball.

**The ball** was caught by Noah.

## Clauses

We're happy.

# Sentences

A **sentence** is a group of words that make sense on their own. A sentence might give information or ask a question. A sentence always begins with a capital letter, and it ends with a full stop, a question mark or an exclamation mark.

Look at these words, and see how they become a sentence.

Giraffes

Giraffes
have

Giraffes
have
long

Giraffes
have
long
necks.

I want to

I want to
travel to

I want to
travel to
the Moon

I want to travel
to the Moon in
a rocket.

All sentences **must** have a verb. You can't make a sentence without a verb because the verb tells us what happens.

I football
every day.

I play
football
every day.

Snakes
along the
ground.

Snakes
slither
along the
ground.

Most sentences have a subject, which tells us who does the action of the verb.

Cheetahs run fast.
subject / verb

Beetles scuttle along.
subject / verb

The person or thing that comes after the verb is called the object. The object receives the action of the verb.

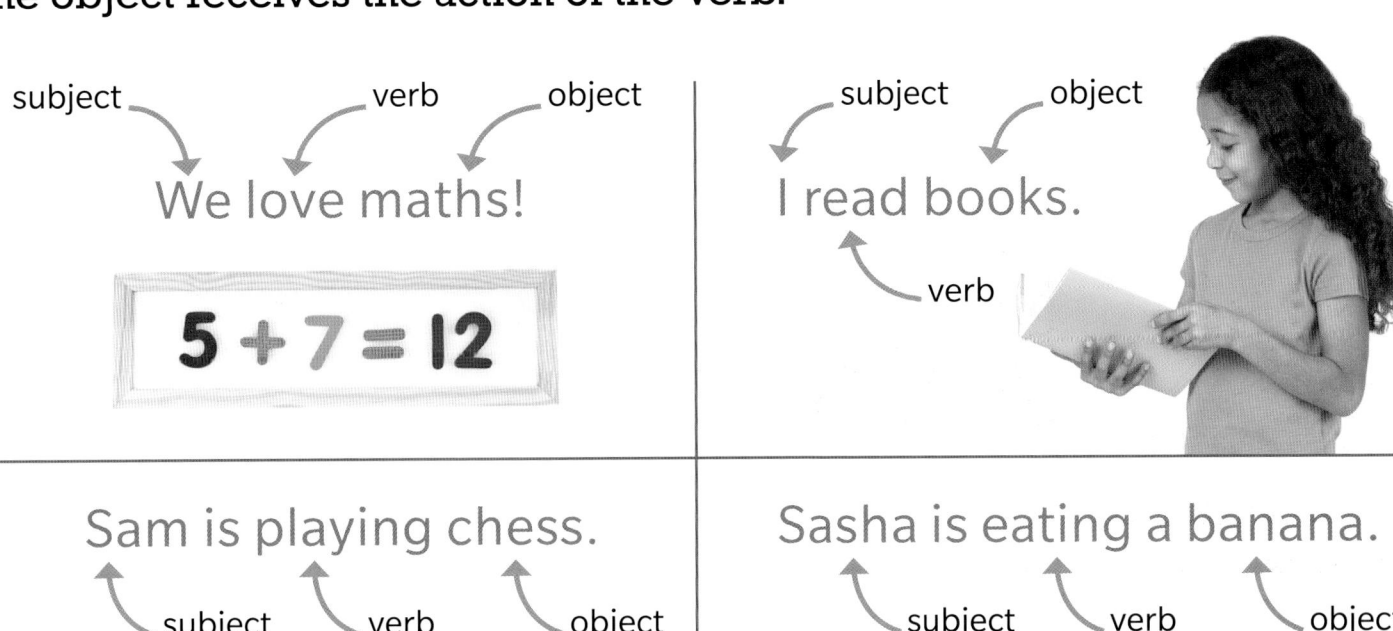

subject / verb / object
We love maths!

$$5 + 7 = 12$$

subject / object
I read books.
verb

Sam is playing chess.
subject / verb / object

Sasha is eating a banana.
subject / verb / object

# Statements

A **statement** is a sentence that gives us information or tells part of a story. It starts with a capital letter and ends with a full stop.

These statements give us information.

Giant pandas eat bamboo.

Pumpkins are tasty, and you can also use them to make lanterns.

These statements tell part of a story.

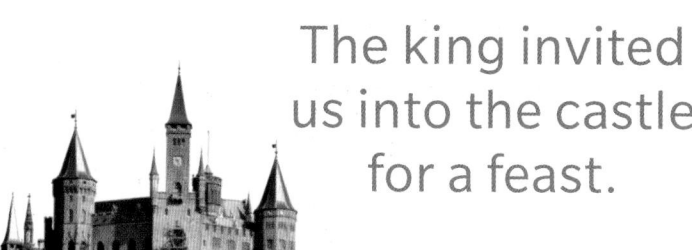

The king invited us into the castle for a feast.

Dan looked at the treasure map excitedly.

You can also end a statement with an exclamation mark (!), to make it sound more exciting.

I scored three goals today!

We ran back to the helicopter, but the engine wouldn't start!

# Questions

A **question** is a sentence that asks something. It starts with a capital letter and ends with a question mark (?).

Is that your guinea pig?

Do you like oranges?

We often use words like **who**, **what**, **which**, **where**, **why**, **how**, **when** and **whose** in questions.

What have you got in your lunch box?

Who wants to play basketball with me?

Why are your shoes so dirty?

Where do polar bears live?

**Top tip**
You can use questions when you are writing a story, to create a feeling of mystery. For example,
**I picked up the old box. What was inside it?**

# Exclamations

An **exclamation** is a sentence that begins with **What** or **How**. It expresses a strong feeling of happiness, surprise, anger or fear. It starts with a capital letter and ends with an exclamation mark.

What beautiful flowers!

What big claws it's got!

What an amazing cave!

How scary!

How cute they are!

How delicious that meal looks!

**Top tip**
You can also use an exclamation mark at the end of a statement to make it sound more exciting. For example, **We drove really fast!** This is still a statement, not an exclamation, because exclamations always begin with **What** or **How**.

# Commands

A **command** is a sentence that tells someone to do something. It starts with a capital letter and can end with a full stop or an exclamation mark.

Some commands are instructions.

Mix the flour and the butter.

Glue the patterned paper onto your picture.

We use an exclamation mark when someone says a command loudly or gives an order.

Be careful!

Sit!

Slow down!

Don't eat all our nuts!

# Noun phrases

Nouns are the names of things, animals and people, such as **tree**, **tiger** and **brother**. A **noun phrase** is a group of words that all belong with the noun and tell us more about it.

Look at how we can add words to the noun **dog** to make a noun phrase that describes what the dog is like.

a small dog

a small white dog with a little orange collar

a small white dog with a little orange collar and a flowing cape

A noun phrase is not a sentence. It doesn't begin with a capital letter and end with a full stop. It just gives more information about a noun. In a sentence, we can use a noun phrase like a noun.

 We saw a ship.

 We saw **an old sailing ship with three tall masts**.

**Top tip**

Using longer noun phrases can make your writing more interesting.

# Prepositional phrases

Prepositions are words such as **on**, **in**, **to** and **with**. Prepositions are always followed by a noun or pronoun. A **prepositional phrase** is the preposition and the following noun or pronoun together.

There are some fish **in the water**.

She slid **down the slide**.

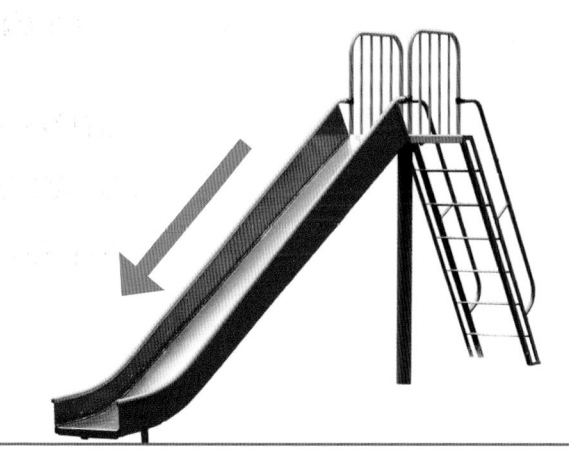

The cat jumped **onto my lap**.

I like pizza **with cheese and tomato**.

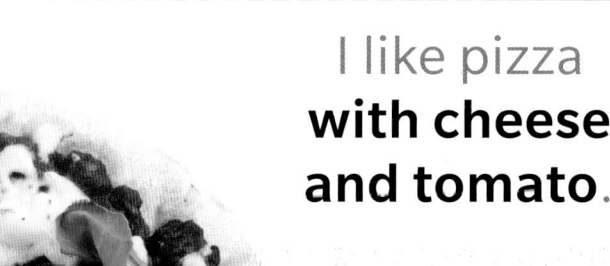

I got a new toy **for my birthday**.

I went to bed **at eleven o'clock**!

# Adverbials

**Adverbials** do the same job as adverbs. They describe **how**, **why**, **when** or **where** something happens. While adverbs are always one word, adverbials can be one word or several words.

These adverbials tell us **how** something happens:

The rabbit appeared **magically**.

It appeared **as if by magic**.

He fought **bravely**.

He fought **with great courage**.

These adverbials tell us **where** or **when** something happens:

Kitty's hiding **over there**.

She's hiding **behind the bag**.

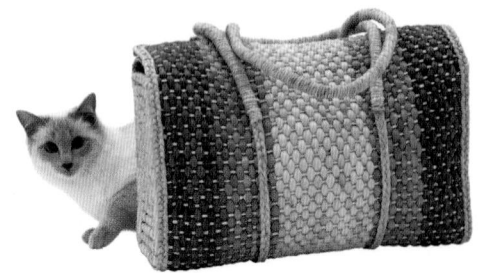

It's my birthday **tomorrow**.

It's my birthday **on the tenth of July**.

**Top tip**

Adverbials answer these questions:
**How? When? Why? Where?**

# Fronted adverbials

Adverbials often come at the end of a sentence. However, you can put them at the beginning of a sentence if they're important and you want them to stand out. These are called **fronted adverbials**.

**Once upon a time**, there was a lion cub called Larry.

**Every weekday**, we go to school on the bus.

**Slowly and cautiously**, Tabitha opened the door and went inside.

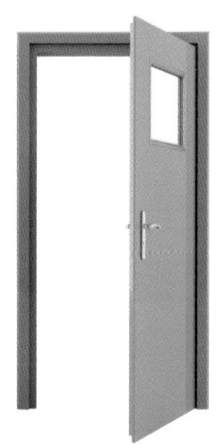

**As quickly as I could**, I put on my spacesuit and got ready for my spacewalk.

**Finally**, it was time to open my presents!

**Actually**, it's a koala, not a bear!

# Clauses

Verbs are words that tell you what someone or something does, such as **sing**, **go** and **play**. A **clause** is a group of words that contains a verb.

we play indoors

it's snowing

he is happy

I'm going on holiday

Some clauses can also be a sentence on their own, if you give them a capital letter and a full stop.

We're happy.

It's snowing!

You can put clauses together to make longer sentences. To do this, you add a word to join the two clauses together. You join clauses together with **conjunctions**.

We play indoors **when** it's snowing.

He is happy **because** he's going on holiday.

There are different ways to join clauses together in a sentence.

the magician waved his wand + the prince turned into a frog

The magician waved his wand **and** the prince turned into a frog.

The prince turned into a frog **as soon as** the magician waved his wand.

kangaroos can jump far + they have powerful back legs

Kangaroos can jump far **because** they have powerful back legs.

Kangaroos have powerful back legs **so** they can jump far.

# Main clauses

A **main clause** is a clause that makes sense on its own, so it also works as a sentence on its own. All sentences must have at least one main clause.

**I got a kite for my birthday**, so I went to the park.

This is a main clause because it could be a sentence on its own.

This is not a main clause because it doesn't make sense on its own.

**I was terrified** when I saw the spider.

The main clause doesn't have to come first in the sentence.

As soon as it was dark, **the badger set off to find food**.

This is not a main clause.

This is a main clause.

Because it was hot, **we stayed in the shade**.

This is not a main clause.

This is a main clause.

**Top tip**
If a clause is a main clause, you can make it into a sentence on its own.

We use conjunctions to link clauses together. The conjunctions **and**, **but** and **or** are called coordinating conjunctions. When we use these conjunctions to join clauses, we say that both clauses are main clauses. In these sentences, both the underlined clauses are main clauses.

**It's raining** and **I'm happy**!

**I like tennis** and **I like basketball**.

**We opened the chest**, but **it was empty**.

**I read a book**, but **then I lost it**.

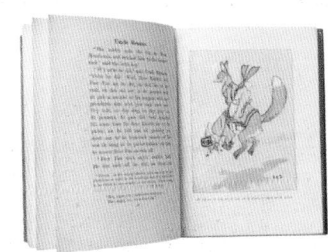

**Meerkats eat insects** or **they sometimes eat snakes' eggs**.

**We can play the guitar** or **we can bang on the drums**.

# Subordinate clauses

A clause that doesn't make sense on its own is called a **subordinate clause**. Subordinate clauses often begin with conjunctions such as **after**, **before**, **because**, **as**, **when**, **while**, **if**, **since** and **although**. These conjunctions are called **subordinating conjunctions**.

I was amazed **when I saw all the presents**.

We'll be late for school **if we don't hurry**!

Charley's excited **because it's time for his walk**.

I always clean my teeth **before I go to bed**.

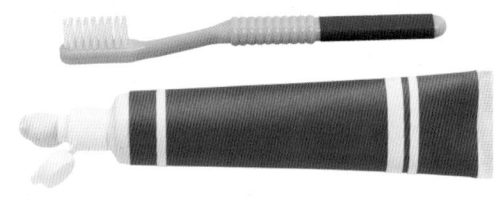

Sometimes a subordinate clause can come first in a sentence.

**Although they are small**, bees do a very important job.

**While I was waiting**, I played a game.

# Relative clauses

Sometimes you might want to add more information about someone or something that you are talking about. To join this extra information into one sentence, you can use a **relative clause**. Relative clauses often begin with **who**, **which** or **that**.

astronauts are people + they go into space

Astronauts are people **who go into space**.

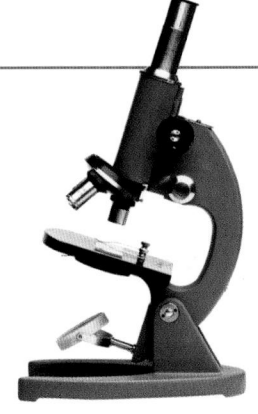

scientists often use microscopes + they make tiny things look bigger

Scientists often use microscopes, **which make tiny things look bigger**.

dinosaurs were huge creatures + they lived millions of years ago

Dinosaurs were huge creatures **that lived millions of years ago**.

You can also use a relative clause to make a comment about a whole idea and give your opinion.

I'm going to be in a play, **which is exciting**!

# Relative pronouns

**Relative pronouns** are words such as **who**, **which**, **that**, **where** and **when**. We use them in relative clauses to add more information about a person or thing.

We use **who** to add more information about people, and we use **which** to add more information about things.

 A magician is a person **who** does magic tricks.

Rhinos live in Africa, **which** is a big continent.

We can use **that** for either people or things.

The player **that** gets the most counters into the hole is the winner.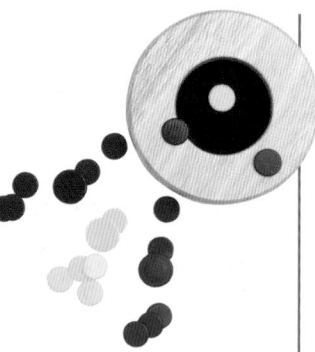

I'm playing on the swing **that** I got for my birthday.

We use **where** to give more information about a place, and **when** to give more information about a time.

Small birds try to find a safe place **where** they can nest.

I can remember the day **when** I started school.

We use **whose** to say who something belongs to.

I played with Dan, **whose** new trampoline is amazing!

It's Dan's trampoline – it belongs to him.

This is Elsie, **whose** cat follows her everywhere.

It's Elsie's cat – it belongs to her.

We can sometimes leave out the relative pronouns **who**, **which** and **that**. We can leave them out when the person or thing we are talking about is the object of a verb. Compare these sentences:

Parrots are birds **that** can learn to talk.

Hello

Parrots are the subject because they can learn to talk. We can't leave out "that".

Parrots are birds ~~that~~ you can teach to talk.

Parrots are the object because we teach them to talk. We can leave out "that".

We sometimes use **whom** in formal writing. We use it when the person we are talking about is the object of a verb. Compare these two sentences:

Here, Max is the subject. → Max is the one **who** loves me true.

Here, Max is the object. → Max is the one **whom** I love too!

**Top tip**

We can never leave out the relative pronouns **where**, **when** or **whose**.

# Active and passive sentences

In **active sentences**, the **doer** of the action comes first.
In **passive sentences**, you can change the order around,
and put the **receiver** of the action first.

This is an active sentence:

**Noah** caught the ball.

This is a passive sentence:

**The ball** was caught by Noah.

Notice that we change the verb in passive sentences.

My sister **made** these cakes.

These cakes **were made** by my sister.

**Remember!**
Active and passive are simple, you see:
If I hit the ball, the ball is hit by me!

We often use passive sentences when we don't know who did the action of the verb.

Some jewels **were stolen** from the castle last night.

My jumper **was made** in America.

We also use the passive if we want to focus on what happened, rather than on who did something.

My boots **have been cleaned**!

Her fur **has been clipped**.

In passive sentences we can add the doer of the action, using **by**.

These paw prints were made **by a dog**.

The first practical telephone was invented **by Alexander Graham Bell**.

# Direct speech

In stories, we often write about what people say to each other. When we write **direct speech**, we write exactly what someone says, and we use inverted commas (speech marks).

"Let's go and find the treasure."

"Look, there's a rainbow!"

 "Is there anyone in there?"

"Go away!"

"There's a shark in the water!"

"It's a secret."

**Top tip** When you use direct speech in your writing, try using lots of different verbs instead of just **said**. Try verbs such as **cried**, **shouted**, **whispered** and **screamed**.

# Reported speech

When we use **reported speech**, we report back what the person said. We don't give their exact words, and we don't use inverted commas (speech marks).

This is direct speech:

"I'm cold."

This is reported speech:

Beth said that she was cold.

"What's in your bag?"

Molly asked me what was in my bag.

"The bouncy castle is amazing!"

Anthony said that the bouncy castle was amazing.

"Where has the hamster gone?"

Oliver asked where the hamster had gone.

# Direct to reported speech

When we change direct speech to reported speech, we have to make some changes to the words we use. If direct speech uses a present tense, we use a past tense in reported speech.

"I **am** hungry."

Krishna said that she **was** hungry.

"The water **is** lovely and warm."

Jayla said that the water **was** lovely and warm.

"The cat **has hurt** his paw."

Poppy said that the cat **had hurt** his paw.

"I **will beat** Harry at chess."

Ali said that he **would beat** Harry at chess.

We also have to change pronouns such as **I**, **he** and **she** in reported speech.

Emily said that **she** loved pasta.

"I love pasta."

"**We** are making cakes."

Daisy and Lucas said that **they** were making cakes.

When you write, try using lots of different verbs to report what people say. It will help make your writing more interesting.

Here are some more verbs you can use in reported speech:

"Fetch!"

Maria **ordered** the dog to fetch the ball.

"Would you like to come to my party?"

Sophie **invited** me to her party.

"It wasn't me."

Jack **denied** breaking the cup.

Liam **promised** to tidy up later.

"I'll tidy up later."

"Let's go to the beach."

Mia **suggested** going to the beach.

Tim **refused** to go to bed.

"I don't want to go to bed!"

# Sentences quiz

Here is a passage from a story for you to read. Then, see if you can answer the questions below. You'll find the answers on the next page.

> Trembling with fear, I approached the wizard's door, which was huge and black. I couldn't turn back now. I lifted the ancient brass knocker and knocked three times. After a while, the door was pulled open. In front of me stood a small, friendly looking boy. I was taken aback, because I was expecting the wizard. "Who are you?" I asked. "I'm Tom, the wizard's assistant," he replied. "How nice to see you! Come in. The wizard's expecting you."

## sentence

I couldn't turn back now.

1. What kind of sentence is this? Is it a statement, a question, an exclamation or a command?
2. How many clauses does the sentence have?
3. Can you find a question, an exclamation and a command in the story?

## adverbials

**trembling with fear**

1. Can you find two more adverbials in the story?
2. Which two adverbials are fronted?

## noun phrases

**the ancient brass knocker**

Can you find another noun phrase in the story?

## main clauses

**I approached the wizard's door**

Can you find three more main clauses in the story?

## subordinate clause

**because I was expecting the wizard**

1. What is the conjunction in this clause?
2. Can you find a relative clause in the story?

## passive verb

**the door was pulled open**

Who pulled the door open?

## direct speech

**"Who are you?" I asked.**

Can you find two examples of direct speech that Tom says?

**Answers**

**sentence 1.** a statement **2.** one **3.** Who are you?; How nice to see you!; Come in. **noun phrases** a small, friendly looking boy **adverbials 1.** three times; after a while **2.** trembling with fear; after a while **main clauses** I lifted the ancient brass knocker; I was taken aback; the door was pulled open **subordinate clause 1.** because **2.** which was huge and black **passive verb** the boy **direct speech** "I'm Tom, the wizard's assistant."; "How nice to see you! Come in. The wizard's expecting you."

**!** What a scary dinosaur!

**,** The balloons are red, yellow, green and blue.

**.** Dr._ _ _ _ _
Dept._ _ _ _

**,** Let's play cards.

**?** Can you ride a bike?

96

For my birthday, I had a chocolate cake – which is my favourite – and lots of other lovely food!

**'s**

Look at the princess**'s** beautiful dress.

**;**

I love flying my kite**;** it goes really high!

# Punctuation

Sam said, "Look at this map."

This car is really fast**:** it can travel at 240 km (150 miles) per hour.

**:**

**"b"**

**–**

a double-decker bus

# Capital letters

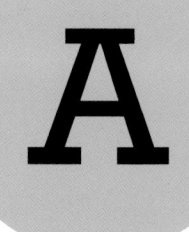

Sentences always begin with a **capital letter**. So a capital letter shows you where a new sentence starts.

**W**e had our sports day last week.
**I**t was fun. **E**veryone enjoyed it.

We use capital letters for the names of people and places.

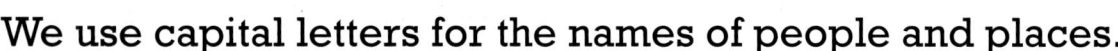

Meet my brother **J**oe and
my sister **A**lice. We were born in
**N**ew **Y**ork **C**ity in the **USA**,
but we now live in **S**ydney, **A**ustralia.

We use capital letters in the titles of books and films, but not for every word.

I'm reading *Charlie and
the Chocolate Factory*.

The names of days of the week and months always start with a capital letter, too.

My birthday is on 12th **S**eptember.
This year, it's on a **S**aturday.

| September | | | | | | |
|---|---|---|---|---|---|---|
| S | M | T | W | T | F | S |
| | | 1 | 2 | 3 | 4 | 5 |
| 6 | 7 | 8 | 9 | 10 | 11 | 12 |
| 13 | 14 | 15 | 16 | 17 | 18 | 19 |
| 20 | 21 | 22 | 23 | 24 | 25 | 26 |
| 27 | 28 | 29 | 30 | | | |

Always use a capital letter when you use the word **I** to talk about yourself.

**I** climbed into the canoe and **I**
started to paddle down the river.

# Full stops

You use a **full stop** at the end of a sentence. It shows that the sentence is finished. Don't forget that after a full stop you need to use a capital letter to start your next sentence.

This is an African elephant. It has a long trunk and big ears. It eats grass, leaves and other vegetation.

You can make really **long sentences** when you write stories by adding lots of exciting **adjectives** and **adverbs** to describe exactly what is happening, but in the end there always has to be a full **STOP**.

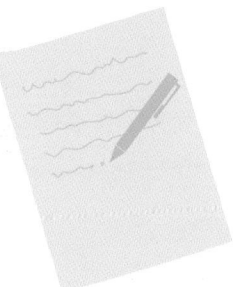

Sometimes a full stop can be used at the end of shortened, or abbreviated, words. But it is also acceptable not to include the full stop.

Dr. stands for "Doctor"

e.g. stands for "for example"

dept. stands for "department"

D.C., in Washington D.C., stands for "District of Columbia"

# Question marks

If you are writing a question, you need to put a **question mark** at the end of the sentence.

Can you ride a bike**?**

Who made these biscuits**?**

How many oranges are there**?**

Where is your rabbit**?**

After a question mark, you need to use a capital letter to start your next sentence.

I looked at the old wooden chest. Who did it belong to**?** What was inside it**?** There was only one way to find out.

# Exclamation marks

!

You can use an **exclamation mark** at the end of a sentence instead of a full stop. An exclamation mark makes a sentence sound more exciting. It suggests that someone is surprised, happy, angry or scared. It can also suggest that someone is shouting.

Go away!

What a scary dinosaur!

After an exclamation mark, you need to use a capital letter to start your next sentence.

We won the competition! We were the champions.

What a cute kitten! Can we take her home?

**Top tip**
Try not to use exclamation marks all the time. If you use them occasionally they'll have more impact!

# Commas

You use **commas** to separate different things in a list. You usually use **and** or **or** before the last thing in the list, and you don't usually use a comma before **and** or **or**.

The balloons are red, yellow, green and blue.

You can have an apple, an orange, a banana or some grapes.

You use commas between different clauses in a sentence. The comma separates the different ideas in the sentence and makes the sentence easier to understand.

I'm older than Joaquin, but he's taller than me.

Owls are nocturnal, so they come out at night.

You can also use commas to separate out part of a sentence that is extra information. Notice that you use a comma **before** and **after** the extra information.

Jake, who is in my class, is really good at roller-skating.

Young bears, which are born in the winter, have to learn to find food.

You use a comma before or after someone's name to show that someone is speaking to them.

Come here, Winston!

Mum, can I go on that ride?

You can use a comma to separate two adjectives before a noun.

She's got long, curly hair.

Peacocks have large, colourful tails.

When you start a sentence with an adverb or an adverbial, you use a comma after it, before you begin the main part of the sentence.

Luckily, I still had the magic ring.

Once upon a time, there was a beautiful princess.

**Top tip** When you use commas in direct speech, always put them inside the inverted commas.

# Apostrophes

Sometimes you can join two words together into one word, such as **don't** (do not). These joined words don't include all the letters of both words. You use an **apostrophe** to replace the missing letters.

Guinea pigs **don't** eat meat. ← do not

**We've** ← we have got a new car.

**She's** a very good dancer. ← she is

It **isn't** raining now. is not →

There are some contractions that we would not usually write as separate words. In the past, they were written separately, but today we use contractions.

**Let's** play cards. ← let us

The clock struck **twelve o'clock**. ← twelve of the clock

# Possessive apostrophes

**'s**

You can use an apostrophe with an **-s** to show who something belongs to. This is called a **possessive apostrophe**. If you possess something, you own it.

You can use a possessive apostrophe after someone's name or after a noun.

These are Olivia**'s** shoes.

Those are my dad**'s** glasses.

If you are talking about more than one person or thing, and the noun you are using ends in **-s**, you just add the apostrophe. You don't add another **s**. Compare these sentences:

The chick**'s** feathers are yellow.

The chick**s'** feathers are yellow.

Some nouns end in -**ss** even when you are only talking about one person or thing, and some names end in -**s**. These words add **'s** as usual for possession.

Look at the princess**'s** beautiful dress.

James**'s** new train set is amazing!

# Its or it's

You use **its**, with no apostrophe, to show that something belongs to an animal or a thing.

The dog is wagging **its** tail.

The baby monkey stays close to **its** mother.

The baby snake is coming out of **its** shell.

The bird is sitting on **its** eggs in **its** nest.

This bucket has lost **its** handle.

I can't play this now because **its** strings are broken.

**It's** is a short form of **it is** or **it has**. The apostrophe replaces the missing letters.

Look! **It's** a starfish!

*it is*

**It's** raining!

*it is*

Where's the rabbit?
**It's** in the hat!

*it is*

Where is my scarf?
**It's** disappeared!

*it has*

This is my new coat.
**It's** got wooden toggles.

*it has*

## Remember!

**It's** a mouse, as you can see.
(Please notice the apostrophe.)
**Its** eyes are bright, **its** tail is long.
(Apostrophes here would be wrong!)

# Brackets

You use **brackets** to separate out part of a sentence that is extra information. You put brackets around it to show that it is additional information and isn't the most important thing you are saying. The rest of the sentence should still make sense if you take out the part in brackets.

Look at how you can add extra information to these sentences using brackets:

We saw a deer in the forest.

We saw a deer (and lots of rabbits) in the forest.

My new kitten is really cute.

My new kitten (white with pink paws) is really cute.

When you are telling a story, you can use brackets to add your opinion about the story.

For dinner, we had spaghetti (which is my favourite).

We played on Sophie's new trampoline (which was amazing).

**Top tip** You can also use commas and dashes instead of brackets to add extra information.

# Inverted commas

We often write about what people say to each other. When we write someone's exact words, we use **inverted commas**. They are also called speech marks.

The words inside inverted commas always start with a capital letter. The person who says the words can come before or after the words themselves.

Sam said, **"**Look at this map.**"**

**"**Look at this map,**"** Sam said.

In the sentences below, the person who says the words comes first. Notice that we add a comma **before** the inverted commas. The speech inside the inverted commas can end with a full stop, a question mark or an exclamation mark. This always comes **inside** the inverted commas.

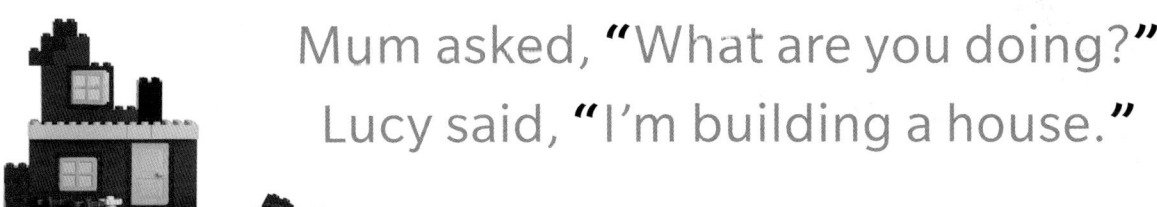

Mum asked, **"**What are you doing?**"**

Lucy said, **"**I'm building a house.**"**

The rules are slightly different if the person who says the words comes **after** the inverted commas. The speech inside the inverted commas still begins with a capital letter, and it still ends with a comma, a question mark or an exclamation mark. However, it shouldn't end with a full stop.

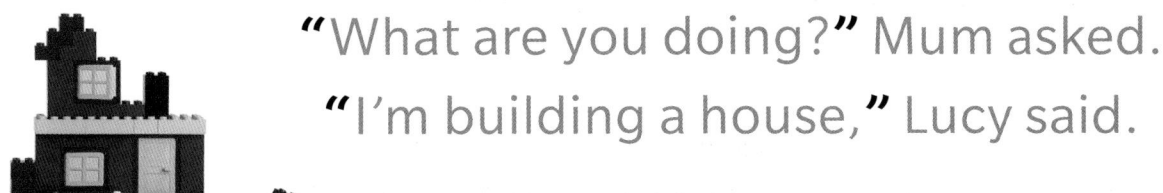

**"**What are you doing?**"** Mum asked.

**"**I'm building a house,**"** Lucy said.

# Dashes

You can use a **dash** to separate one part of the sentence from the rest. You often use a dash to add an extra comment or an opinion at the end of a sentence.

We were feeling quite cheerful and enjoying the picnic – until it started to rain!

Patch finally came home two hours later – very wet and muddy!

I got a mini helicopter for my birthday – it's amazing!

Tara's got a pet hamster – it's so cute!

You can also use dashes like brackets to separate out part of a sentence that is extra information.

I can play *Happy Birthday to You* – and a few other tunes – on the keyboard.

For my birthday, I had a chocolate cake – which is my favourite – and lots of other lovely food!

# Hyphens

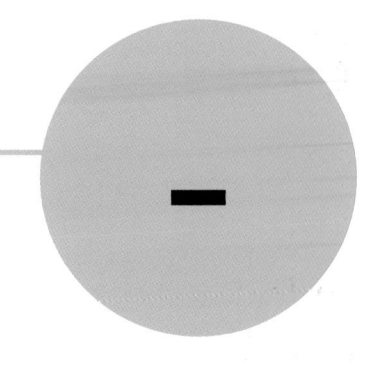

You use **hyphens** to join words together to make them into a single word. You can also use them to link words together to make the meaning very clear. When you write a hyphen, it is shorter than a dash.

a double-decker bus

a seven-year-old boy

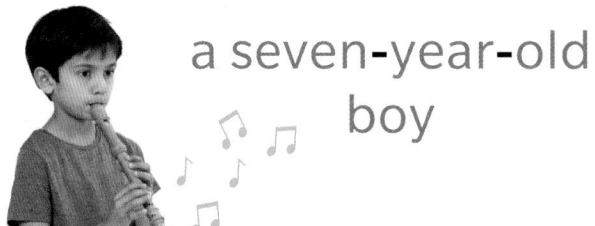

a long-haired guinea pig

a man-eating shark

You can also use hyphens to create your own new words.

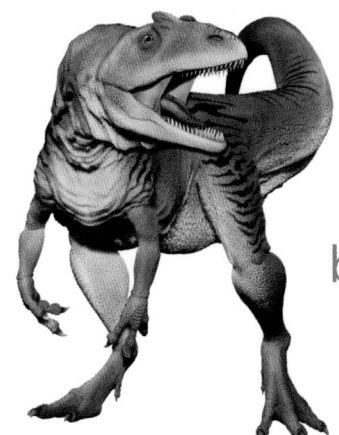

a dinosaur with huge, bone-crushing teeth

This is my special ghost-hunting torch.

**Top tip** We use hyphens in numbers such as twenty-three, thirty-five or ninety-nine.

# Colons

You use a **colon** to introduce a list. You can also use a colon to join two ideas together into one sentence.

You use a colon to introduce a list.

My favourite sports are: hockey, basketball and tennis.

To go camping, you need: a tent, a stove for cooking and a sleeping bag.

These are my friends: Ellie, Rohan and Sarah.

I've got three pets: a hamster, a guinea pig and a new kitten.

You can also use a colon to join two ideas together into one sentence. You use a colon when the second idea explains the first idea.

Lions are predators: they hunt and kill other animals for food.

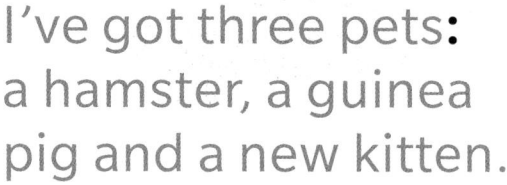

This car is really fast: it can travel at 240 km (150 miles) per hour.

**Top tip** Never use a capital letter after a colon unless it's the first letter of a proper noun.

# Semi-colons

You can use a **semi-colon** to join two ideas together into one sentence to show that the ideas are closely linked. Never use a capital letter after a semi-colon unless it's the first letter of a proper noun.

There are lots of monkeys in the safari park; there are elephants and giraffes, too.

I love flying my kite; it goes really high!

My uncle can make animals out of balloons; he's going to teach me how to do it.

I've never been on a plane before; I'm really excited!

You can also use semi-colons instead of commas to separate different things in a list. It's best to use semi-colons when each thing on the list is quite long and complicated.

To make your monster mask, you will need: a large piece of plain card; paints and brushes; a small pot of glitter; scissors and glue.

113

# Ellipses

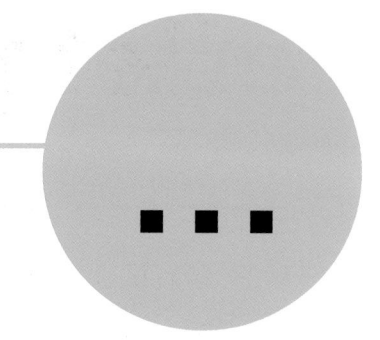

You can use three dots, called an **ellipsis**, to show that a sentence is not finished. We often use an ellipsis to suggest that there is more to say about something.

You can use an ellipsis to add suspense.

With my heart thumping in my chest, I gradually climbed up the steps towards the castle ...

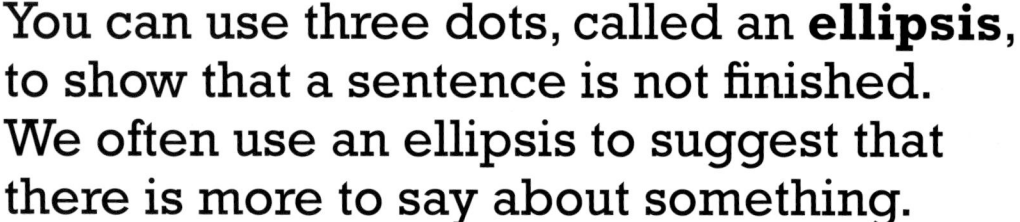

I found William's bike and helmet in the park, but there was no sign of him. Something was wrong ...

You can use an ellipsis to show that someone pauses when they are speaking.

"We've got water and some fruit, so ... what else do we need for our picnic?"

"I found this key in the shed, but ... I don't think it's the right one."

You can also use an ellipsis to show that some numbers are missing in a sequence. You might use it so that you don't have to write all the numbers.

1, 2, 3 ... 10

10, 20, 30 ... 100

# Bullet points

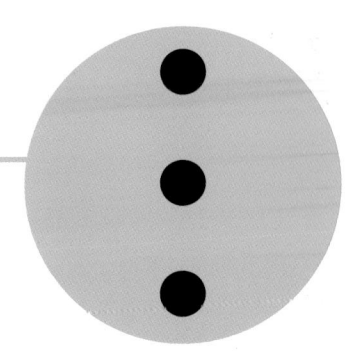

To help you organize things in a list, you can use bullet points. We use a colon before a list, to introduce it.

My packing list:
- clothes
- mask and snorkel
- flip flops
- games

Things to do:
- tidy my room
- write party invitations
- do homework
- go ice-skating (Hooray!)

Sometimes the things on the list can be full sentences, so they have a capital letter and a full stop.

Reasons to get a puppy:
- I will enjoy taking it for walks.
- It will be fun to play with.
- I will learn how to look after an animal.

Some advantages of technology:
- You can message people.
- You can learn things on the Internet.
- You can play games.

**Top tip**  Bullet points can be different shapes – you might try star shapes instead of points!

# Punctuation quiz

Here is a passage from a story for you to read. Then, see if you can answer the questions.

Ben and I called Detective Brown and then stayed close behind as he and his partner followed the robbers back to their house (a small house near the park). As we watched from a distance, we saw that the robbers were inside, and were taking things out of their large, black bag: money, jewellery and expensive-looking watches – all the things they had stolen earlier. Suddenly, Ben gasped. "What's the matter?" I asked. "Look," he whispered. "There! That's Grandma's purse!" We looked at each other and smiled; we couldn't wait to see Grandma's face when we told her we'd found her purse ...

## capital letters A

As  Suddenly

1. Why are capital letters used in these words?
2. Can you find four capital letters used in the characters' names?

## inverted commas "b"

"What's the matter?"

What do the inverted commas show?

## question marks ?

What's the matter?

Is the question mark inside or outside the inverted commas?

## exclamation marks !

That's Grandma's purse!

Why is there an exclamation mark here?

## full stops

·

... I asked.

1. How many more full stops can you find?
2. What is there at the end of the story, instead of a full stop? What does it suggest?

## commas

,

As we watched from a safe distance, we ...

1. What does this comma separate?
2. Can you find a comma in a list, and a comma between two adjectives?

## colons

:

they started taking things out of their bag: money, jewellery and expensive-looking watches

What does the colon introduce?

## brackets

(b)

(a small house near the park)

Why are there brackets here?

## apostrophes

's

What's the matter?

1. What does the apostrophe replace here?
2. Can you find two possessive apostrophes?

## hyphens and dashes

-

expensive-looking

1. Why is there a hyphen here?
2. Can you find a dash – is it longer or shorter than a hyphen?
3. Why is it there?

Answers

capital letters 1. because they are at the beginning of a sentence 2. Ben, Grandma, Detective Brown inverted commas direct speech – it is exactly what someone said question marks inside exclamation marks to show that something exciting is happening full stops 1. four 2. ellipses ... It suggests that there is more to say commas 1. two clauses 2. money, jewellery and expensive-looking watches; their large, black bag colons a list of things brackets because it's extra information apostrophes 1. the letter "i" (what is) 2. Grandma's purse, Grandma's face hyphens and dashes 1. to join the two words together 2. watches – all the things they had stolen earlier; longer 3. to introduce extra information

# Writing tips

Here is a passage from a story for you to read, together with tips for how grammar and punctuation can help you improve your writing.

As quickly as we could, we climbed into the rowing boat and rowed ashore. We dragged the boat ashore and tied it securely to a tree. We knew we didn't have long. The pirates had gone back to their ship for supplies, but they would be back soon. Annie took the map out of her pocket and pointed to some large, jagged rocks in the distance. "Over there," she said excitedly. "That's where the treasure's buried!"

## conjunctions

Use conjunctions to link clauses together and make longer sentences.

The pirates had gone back to their ship for supplies, **but** they would be back soon.

## descriptive noun phrases

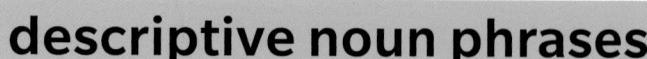

Use descriptive noun phrases to add more detail to nouns.

**some large, jagged rocks** in the distance

## past perfect

Use the past perfect for things that happened earlier.

The pirates **had gone** back to their ship

## pronouns

Use pronouns so you don't keep repeating the same nouns.

**We** dragged the boat ashore and tied **it** securely to a tree.

## direct speech

Be careful with the punctuation of direct speech.

"Over there**,"** she said excitedly.

## adjectives and adverbs

Use interesting adjectives and adverbs.

jagged, securely, excitedly

## adverbial

Fronting an adverbial emphasizes it and makes it stand out more.

**As quickly as we could**, we climbed into the rowing boat

## exclamation marks

Use exclamation marks (but not too many) to create excitement.

That's where the treasure's buried**!**

# Common mistakes in grammar

It's easy to make mistakes with grammar!
Here are a few things to watch out for.

**It's** means **it is** or **it has**. **Its** shows that something belongs to an animal or an object.

☑ Look, **it's** a
polar bear.

☒ Look, **its** a
polar bear.

☑ This monkey is using
**its** tail to hold on!

☒ This monkey is using
**it's** tail to hold on!

**They're** means **they are**. We use **there** to refer to a place. **Their** means belonging to them.

☑ Look at the ducks. **They're**
swimming on the lake. They
use **their** feet to paddle.

☒ Look at the ducks. **There**
swimming on the lake. They
use **they're** feet to paddle.

☑ **There** are some
conkers over **there**.

☒ **They're** are some
conkers over **their**.

**We're** means **we are**. **Were** is the past tense of the verb be.

☑ Yesterday we
**were** at school.

☒ Yesterday we
**we're** at school.

☑ **We're** on holiday now!

☒ **Were** on holiday now!

**Who's** means **who is** or **who has**. You use **whose** to ask who something belongs to.

- ☑ **Who's** coming to your party?
- ☒ **Whose** coming to your party?

- ☑ **Whose** shoes are these?
- ☒ **Who's** shoes are these?

---

You use **what** to ask questions. You use **that** in relative clauses.

**What** are those? Are they lychees?

- ☑ This is a fruit salad **that** I made.
- ☒ This is a fruit salad **what** I made.

---

**You're** means **you are**. **Your** things are the things that belong to you.

- ☑ **You're** good at drawing.
- ☒ **Your** good at drawing.

- ☑ Are these **your** pencils?
- ☒ Are these **you're** pencils?

---

**He's** means **he is**. **His** things belong to him.

- ☑ **He's** my brother.
- ☒ **His** my brother.

Dan is riding **his** new bike.

# Common mistakes in punctuation

It's easy to make mistakes with punctuation! Here are a few things to watch out for.

Always use a capital letter at the beginning of a sentence, for names (proper nouns) and for the pronoun **I**.

☑ **G**iraffes live in **A**frica.

☒ **g**iraffes live in **a**frica.

 ☑ This is a present **I** bought for **A**rjun.

☒ This is a present **i** bought for **a**rjun.

Don't use a capital letter after a colon or a semi-colon (unless it's a proper noun or the pronoun **I**).

☑ He showed me what was in his pencil case: **p**encils, pens and a rubber.

☒ He showed me what was in his pencil case: **P**encils, pens and a rubber.

☑ Our dog is always muddy; **s**he loves playing in the garden!

☒ Our dog is always muddy; **S**he loves playing in the garden!

Use an apostrophe to show possession, and remember to put it in the correct place.

**Singular**

☑ my brother**'s** trainers

☒ my brother**s'** trainers

**Plural**

☑ my brother**s'** trainers

☒ my brother**'s** trainers

Use a comma between adjectives, when they come before a noun.

- ☑ a beautiful, colourful bird
- ☒ a beautiful colourful bird

- ☑ a huge, terrifying dinosaur
- ☒ a huge terrifying dinosaur

Always use a capital letter at the beginning of direct speech. Don't forget to put a punctuation mark at the end, inside the inverted commas.

- ☑ "Let's play on the swings," Zara said.
- ☒ "Let's play on the swings", Zara said.

- ☑ "This is fun!" Charlie shouted.
- ☒ "This is fun"! Charlie shouted.

You can use brackets for adding extra information. The full stop usually goes after brackets, but it goes inside the brackets if the information in the brackets is a full sentence.

- ☑ I love those shoes (the red ones).
- ☒ I love those shoes (the red ones.)

- ☑ I've always wanted a hamster. (My mum has always refused to buy me one.)
- ☒ I've always wanted a hamster. (My mum has always refused to buy me one).

# Glossary

**abstract noun** Type of noun that is the name of a feeling or idea *anger, happiness, fear*

**adjective** Word that describes a noun *tall, clever, beautiful, green, happy*

**adverb** Word that describes how, when or where you do something *quickly, slowly, soon, now, then, here, there*

**adverbial** Word or group of words that do the same job as an adverb and tell you how, when or where something happens *after a while, all at once, on the fifth of June, over there, as quickly as I could*

**adverb of manner** Type of adverb that describes how you do something *carefully, dangerously, immediately, badly, well*

**adverb of place** Type of adverb that describes where something happens *here, there, everywhere, indoors, upstairs*

**adverb of time** Type of adverb that describes when something happens *today, yesterday, now, later*

**apostrophe** Punctuation mark that you use to show that a letter is missing, or to show possession *there's, she's, it's, Jack's*

**auxiliary verb** Type of verb that you use to help you form different tenses *We are playing. We have finished. I don't like cheese.*

**brackets** Punctuation marks that you use to separate out part of a sentence that has extra information *I went to the park with George (he's my best friend) and Chloe.*

**bullet points** Small round punctuation marks that you use to list things one below the other

**capital letter** Big form of a letter that you use at the beginning of a sentence or for names *A, B, C*

**clause** Group of words that contains a verb *I live in London, that's my dog*

**collective noun** Type of noun that refers to a group of animals, people or things *a flock of sheep, a crowd of people*

**colon** Punctuation mark that you use to introduce a list *I love sports: tennis, football, basketball and hockey.*

**comma** Punctuation mark that you use between clauses, in lists and between adjectives *We finished our food, then we went home. I'm going to invite Sam, Anna and Toby. We found an old, wooden chest.*

**command** Type of sentence that tells someone to do something *Sit down! Come here.*

**comparative** Form of an adjective that you use for comparing two things or people *taller, bigger, more important, better, worse*

**compound noun** Type of noun that is formed when two other nouns are put together *toothbrush, fingernail*

**conjunction** Word that joins clauses together *and, but, so, because*

**coordinating conjunction** Word that joins two main clauses together *and, but, or*

**dash** Punctuation mark that you use to separate one part of a sentence *Sophie looked really happy – I don't know why!*

**determiner** Word that goes before a noun to tell you which one you are talking about *this, that, my, your, one, two*

**direct speech** Words that someone actually says *"Stop!" she shouted.*

**ellipses** Punctuation mark that you use to show a sentence is not finished *There was no time to lose …*

**exclamation** Type of sentence that begins with "How" or "What" and says something with a lot of feeling *How amazing! What a strange animal!*

**exclamation mark** Punctuation mark that you use at the end of an exclamation or a sentence to suggest that someone is excited, surprised or angry, or that they are shouting *Look – a ghost! Go away!*

**fronted adverbial** Adverbial that is moved to the front of a sentence, to make it stand out more *All at once, the door flew open. Once upon a time, there was a beautiful princess.*

**full stop** Punctuation mark that you use at the end of a sentence *My name's Adam.*

**future** Forms of verbs that refer to things that will happen one day *I will go to school tomorrow. I may invite some friends for tea. We're going to build a sandcastle.*

**grammar** Way in which you put words together into sentences so that they make sense

**helping verb** Another name for an **auxiliary verb**

**hyphen** Punctuation mark that you use to join two words together *a three-eyed monster, a ten-year-old boy, a dark-haired girl*

**infinitive** Basic form of a verb that hasn't been changed to form different tenses *make, sing, go*

**interjection** Word that you can use to make a sentence on its own *Wow! Hello. Hooray!*

**inverted commas** Punctuation marks that you put around direct speech *"I'm sorry," he said.*

**main clause** Clause that carries the main meaning in a sentence *Dan was happy because there was no school. The film was finished, so we went home.*

**modal verb** Verb that you use in front of an infinitive of another verb to express possibility, ability, or duty *will, might, may, can, could, should, must*

**noun** Word that is the name of a thing, animal, or person *ball, apple, dog, horse, brother*

**noun phrase** Group of words that go with a noun and add more information about it *an old man, a black dog with white paws*

**object** Person or thing that receives the action of a verb *I hit the ball. She ate an apple.*

**part of speech** Type of word *noun, verb, adjective, adverb, determiner*

**passive** Form of a verb in which the receiver of the action comes before the verb *All the food was eaten. The money was stolen from the bank.*

**past perfect** Form of a verb that refers to something that happened earlier in a story *My friends had warned me not to get involved. Someone had eaten all the cake.*

**past tense** Form of a verb that refers to something that happened in the past *played, enjoyed, ate, won, went*

**past progressive** Form of a verb that refers to something in progress in the past *We were playing tennis when it started to rain.*

**plural** Form of a noun that refers to more than one thing, person or animal *books, toys, dogs, children*

**possessive pronoun** Pronoun that tells you who something belongs to *mine, yours, his, hers*

**preposition** Word that links a noun into a sentence *in, at, on, of, for*

**preposition of place** Preposition that tells you where something is *in the box, under the table*

**preposition of time** Preposition that tells you when something happens *on Monday, in the summer, at six o'clock*

**prepositional phrase** Preposition and the noun or pronoun that follows it *in the garden, with a ball*

**present perfect** Form of a verb that refers to something in the past that still has an effect now *I've lost my phone. He's cut his knee.*

**present progressive** Form of a verb that refers to something in progress in the present *I'm doing my homework. We're playing on the computer.*

**pronoun** Word that you use instead of a noun *I, you, he, she, it, we, they*

**proper noun** Noun that is the name of a person or place *Rosa, Eve, Adam, London, New York*

**punctuation** Marks that you use in writing to tell the reader when to pause, when something is a question, when something is shouted, etc. *?, !, " " ( )*

**question** Type of sentence that asks for information *Where do you live? Are you OK?*

**question mark** Punctuation mark that you use at the end of a question *What's that?*

**relative clause** Clause that adds more information about a noun *Sam showed me the bike that he got for his birthday. My sister has a friend who can juggle.*

**relative pronoun** Word that introduces a relative clause *a boy who likes tennis, a dog that bites, the place where we do drama*

**reported speech** Words that report what someone says, without using direct speech *Dan told me that he was tired. She asked me what I was doing.*

**reporting verb** Verb that you use in reported speech *say, tell, ask, warn, order, promise*

**semi-colon** Punctuation mark you can use instead of a full stop, if sentences are closely linked *The party was great; we all enjoyed it.*

**sentence** Group of words that include a verb and make sense on their own. *We watched a film. It's raining.*

**singular** Form of a noun that refers to just one thing, person or animal *bird, pen, computer, girl, mother*

**speech marks** Another word for **inverted commas**

**statement** Type of sentence that gives information *My name's Molly. Lions are big cats.*

**subject** Person or thing that does the action of a verb *Olivia plays the recorder. Horses eat grass.*

**subordinate clause** Clause that is not a main clause and is introduced by a subordinating conjunction *I went indoors, because I was cold. Although he's quite short, Ali is good at basketball.*

**subordinating conjunction** Word that introduces a subordinate clause *because, so, although*

**superlative** Form of an adjective that you use for comparing three or more things or people *biggest, funniest, most exciting, best, worst*

**tense** Form of a verb that tells you whether something happens in the past, present or future *play, played, is playing, was playing, will play*

**verb** Word that describes an action and tells you what a person or thing does *eat, run, sing, play, ride*

# Index

# Acknowledgements

The publisher would like to thank the following people for their help in the production of this book:
Jolyon Goddard (additional editing and proofreading), Chris Fraser and Ann Cannings (additional design), Helen Peters (index).

**Picture credits**
The publisher would like to thank the following for their kind permission to reproduce their photographs:

Key: a=above; c=centre; b=below; l=left; r=right; t=top.

**3 Alamy Stock Photo:** D. Hurst (clb). **4 Alamy Stock Photo:** redbrickstock.com (cl). **9 Dorling Kindersley:** Durham University Oriental Museum (bc/Eighty drachma); The University of Aberdeen (fbl, bl, bc). **10 Dreamstime.com:** Isselee (crb). **11 Alamy Stock Photo:** Krys Bailey (clb). **Dreamstime.com:** Dmitry Kalinovsky (br); Neil Burton (cra). **12 123RF.com:** Sergii Kolesnyk / givaga (cla). **13 123RF.com:** Viachaslau Bondarau (cl). **Dreamstime.com:** Andrey Popov (cra); Nataliia Prokofyeva (cla). **14 123RF.com:** PaylessImages (cb). **15 Dorling Kindersley:** Paul Wilkinson (bl). **Dreamstime.com:** Photoeuphoria (crb). **Fotolia:** Pei Ling Hoo (br). **17 123RF.com:** donatas1205 (clb). **Dreamstime.com:** Francesco Alessi (bl); Kenishirotie (fbl); Matthew Egginton (bl/Mixed Coin). **Getty Images:** Foodcollection (cra). **18 Dorling Kindersley:** Stephen Oliver (cra). **Fotolia:** Ruth Black (clb). **19 Dreamstime.com:** Chris Van Lennep (clb); Derrick Neill (bl). **20 123RF.com:** Roman Gorielov (cra). **Dorling Kindersley:** Jerry Young (br). **Fotolia:** Pekka Jaakkola / Luminis (clb); Sherri Camp (crb). **21 Dorling Kindersley:** Jerry Young (cla). **Dreamstime.com:** Radu Razvan Gheorghe (cb). **Getty Images:** Technotr (cra); vgajic (bl). **22 123RF.com:** Ilka Erika Szasz-Fabian (cra); mrtwister (bl). **ESA / Hubble:** NASA (br). **23 Dorling Kindersley:** Harvey Stanley (br); Hitachi Rail Europe (clb); Ribble Steam Railway / Science Museum Group (crb); Haynes International Motor Museum (fbr). **24 123RF.com:** Konstantin Kamenetskiy (crb). **26 Dorling Kindersley:** Natural History Museum, London (cb); South of England Rare Breeds Centre, Ashford, Kent (bl). **27 123RF.com:** Serhiy Kobyakov (bc). **Dreamstime.com:** Dmitri Maruta (clb). **Fotolia:** Anyaivanova (cr). **28 123RF.com:** Irina Schmidt (bl). **29 123RF.com:** Luca Mason (cb). **Dreamstime.com:** Akulamatiau (cla); Picsfive (crb). **30 Dreamstime.com:** Cynoclub (clb). **32 Dorling Kindersley:** Peter Anderson (crb). **Dreamstime.com:** Dmitry Kalinovsky (clb); Tamara Bauer (bc); Tashka2000 (br). **33 Dorling Kindersley:** Stuart's Bikes (bl). **Dreamstime.com:** Syda Productions (br); Tinnakorn Srivichai (cra). **Getty Images:** Stocktrek RF (cra). **34 Dreamstime.com:** Duncan Noakes (crb). **35 Alamy Stock Photo:** D. Hurst (cra). **Dreamstime.com:** Viktor Pravdica (ca). **36 123RF.com:** Hongqi Zhang (cb, crb). **37 Dreamstime.com:** Aginger (cl, cr). **39 123RF.com:** Kasto (clb). **40 123RF.com:** stockyimages (bl). **Fotolia:** Thomas Dobner / Dual Aspect (bc). **42 Dorling Kindersley:** Blackpool Zoo, Lancashire, UK (cla). **43 123RF.com:** Alena Ozerova (bl); Oleg Sheremetyev (crb). **44 123RF.com:** federicofoto (clb). **Dorling Kindersley:** Liberty's Owl, Raptor and Reptile Centre, Hampshire, UK (cra). **45 123RF.com:** Alena Ozerova (cb); Anatolii Tsekhmister / tsekhmister (c). **46 123RF.com:** PaylessImages (cr). **Alamy Stock Photo:** Image Source Plus (cl); redbrickstock.com (cra). **Dreamstime.com:** Andrius Aleksandravicius (cb/ Wood game); Showface (cb). **47 Dreamstime.com:** Neil Burton (cr); Wavebreakmedia Ltd (cl). **48 123RF.com:** Vitaly Valua / domenicogelermo (cl). **Dreamstime.com:** Viorel Sima (cr). **49 Dorling Kindersley:** Steve Lyne / Richbourne Kennels (cla). **Dreamstime.com:** Cristina (cra). **50 Alamy Stock Photo:** Marius Graf (clb); Picture Partners (cla); Sergii Figurnyi (br). **Dreamstime.com:** Ramona Smiers (ca). **51 Alamy Stock Photo:** MBI (bl). **52 123RF.com:** Irina Iglina / iglira (cla); svitac (cra). **Dorling Kindersley:** Hitachi Rail Europe (clb, bc); Jerry Young (cb). **53 123RF.com:** bennymarty (cla); smileus (cra). **Dreamstime.com:** Waldru (cr). **54 Alamy Stock Photo:** D. Hurst (c). **Dorling Kindersley:** NASA (cl). **Dreamstime.com:** Alexander Raths (ca); Ron Chapple (cr). **55 Alamy Stock Photo:** Foto Grebler (ca); Zoonar GmbH (cb); tuja66 (cra). **Dreamstime.com:** Mtkang (cr). **56 Fotolia:** Makarov Alexander (cr). **57 123RF.com:** scanrail (cl). **Dreamstime.com:** Sergey Kolesnikov (cla). **58 Dorling Kindersley:** Stuart's Bikes (cb). **Dreamstime.com:** Isselee (crb). **59 Alamy Stock Photo:** Aleksandr Belugin (cla). **Dreamstime.com:** Monkey Business Images (ca). **60 123RF.com:** Mike Price / mhprice (cra). **Alamy Stock Photo:** Zoonar GmbH (bc). **61 Alamy Stock Photo:** LJSphotography (bl). **62 Dreamstime.com:** Georgerudy (cla); Sepy67 (cra); Mihail Degteariov (bl). **63 Alamy Stock Photo:** (cla). **64 123RF.com:** Bonzami Emmanuelle / cynoclub (cb/Red fish); Visarute Angkatavanich / bluehand (crb). **Alamy Stock Photo:** Krys Bailey (cra). **Fotolia:** lucielang (cb). **65 Alamy Stock Photo:** Martin Wierink (cr). **Dreamstime.com:** Irina Papoyan (br). **68 123RF.com:** Eric Isselee / isselee (bl). **69 123RF.com:** tan4ikk (clb). **70 123RF.com:** Eric Isselee / isselee (ca). **Dreamstime.com:** Maigi (cb); Showface (bl, bc). **Fotolia:** Alexey Repka (cb/ Moon). **71 Dreamstime.com:** Stangot (bl); Svetlana Foote (cla). **72 123RF.com:** pashabo (cr). **73 123RF.com:** Eric Isselee / isselee (crb). **75 Alamy Stock Photo:** Oleksiy Maksymenko (bc). **Dreamstime.com:** Jose Manuel Gelpi Diaz (cra); Vetkit (bl). **76 Alamy Stock Photo:** Ernie Jordan (clb, cb). **77 Dreamstime.com:** Esteban Miyahira (cra). **79 123RF.com:** Paolo De Santis / archidea (c). **Dorling Kindersley:** Barnabas Kindersley (cra). **Fotolia:** Eric Isselee (cla, br). **80 123RF.com:** Matthias Ziegler (cl); tan4ikk (bl). **Dreamstime.com:** Paul Maguire (cra). **Fotolia:** Silver (br). **81 123RF.com:** Matthias Ziegler (ca). **82 123RF.com:** mariok (crb). **Alamy Stock Photo:** David Chapman (clb). **83 123RF.com:** Eric Isselee / isselee (clb). **Dreamstime.com:** Limeyrunner (cb). **84 Alamy Stock Photo:** Tetra Images (cra). **Fotolia:** Dusan Zutinic / asiana (bc). **85 Dorling Kindersley:** NASA (cra). **Getty Images:** Thomas Northcut / Photodisc (crb). **86 Dreamstime.com:** Jack Schiffer (cra). **89 Getty Images:** Science & Society Picture Library (bc). **90 Corbis:** (cra). **Dreamstime.com:** Pahham (c). **91 Dreamstime.com:** Lbarn (cb). **93 123RF.com:** Jo Ann Snover (cr). **97 Dreamstime.com:** Douglas W Fry (crb). **98 Dreamstime.com:** Natasnow (cra). **102 123RF.com:** Yury Gubin (bc). **Dorling Kindersley:** Liberty's Owl, Raptor and Reptile Centre, Hampshire, UK (crb). **103 123RF.com:** svitlana10 (cra). **106 Getty Images:** claudio.arnese (br). **107 Fotolia:** Kayros Studio (cr). **108 123RF.com:** Katarzyna Białasiewicz (crb). **110 123RF.com:** Denys Prokofyev (br); foodandmore (cla); kokodrill (cra). **111 123RF.com:** Andreas Meyer / digital (cr). **Fotolia:** Matthew Cole (crb). **112 123RF.com:** Anton Starikov (cra). **Dreamstime.com:** Douglas W Fry (crb); Rmarmion (cl). **Photolibrary:** Photodisc / Ryan McVay (cl). **PunchStock:** Westend61 / Rainer Dittrich (crb). **113 123RF.com:** Sefi Greiver (cl). **115 123RF.com:** maraqu (crb). **116 Fotolia:** Matthew Cole (cl). **117 123RF.com:** robodread (crb). **118 PunchStock:** Photodisc (cla, cr). **120 Alamy Stock Photo:** Amazon-Images (cra). **121 Dorling Kindersley:** Gerard Brown / Pedal Pedlar (br). **122 123RF.com:** Brian Jackson (bc); John McAllister (crb); Narmina Gaziyeva (br). **123 123RF.com:** Graham Oliver (cr). **127 Dorling Kindersley:** Ribble Steam Railway / Science Museum Group (br). **128 Fotolia:** Eric Isselee (br)

**Cover images:** *Back:* **123RF.com:** Ilka Erika Szasz-Fabian bl; **Alamy Stock Photo:** D. Hurst cr

All other images © Dorling Kindersley
For further information see: www.dkimages.com